How Two Circuses, Two Countries, and Nine Kids Confront Conflict and Build Community

Cynthia Levinson

PEACHTREE
ATLANTA

Published by
PEACHTREE PUBLISHERS
1700 Chattahoochee Avenue
Atlanta, Georgia 30318-2112
www.peachtree-online.com

Text © 2015 by Cynthia Levinson

Design and composition by Nicola Simmonds Carmack

Text and titles set in Palatino and Bernard MT Condensed

Printed in February 2015 by RR Donnelley & Sons in China
10 9 8 7 6 5 4 3 2 1
First Edition

Library of Congress Cataloging-in-Publication Data

Levinson, Cynthia.
  Watch out for flying kids! / written by Cynthia Levinson. — First Edition.
    pages cm
  ISBN 978-1-56145-821-9
  1. Child acrobats—Biography—Juvenile literature. 2. Child circus performers—
Biography—Juvenile literature. I. Title.
  GV550.L48 2015
  796.47'60922—dc23
  [B]
                              2014018539

With boundless gratitude to Hala Asadi, Hla Asadi,
Sidney ("Iking") Bateman, Shai Ben Yosef, Meghan Clark,
Alexandra Gabliani, Kellin Quinn Hentoff-Killian, Shaina Hughes,
and Roey Shafran, and to Jessica Hentoff and Rabbi Marc Rosenstein.

May you continue to soar.

Salaam سلام
Shalom שלום
Peace
—C. L.

Contents

v

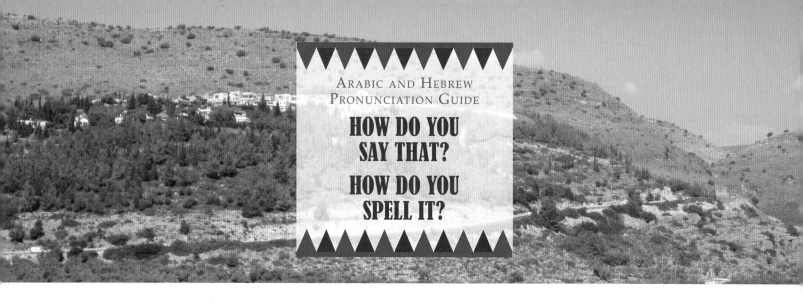

HOW DO YOU SAY THAT?

HOW DO YOU SPELL IT?

A rabic and Hebrew words appear throughout this book. Both are official languages of Israel.

Arabic and Hebrew use two different alphabets; English uses a third. Some letters and sounds in Arabic and Hebrew do not correspond to any letters or sounds in English—or to each other. Transliterating names, words, and sounds from one language to another can be challenging, and translators do not necessarily agree on the best way to spell a word in another language.

This Guide shows the approximate pronunciation of the Arabic and Hebrew names, places, and words and expressions in *Watch Out for Flying Kids*. It also indicates which are Arabic (A), which are Hebrew (H), and which Arabic words have been adopted by Hebrew-speakers (A/H). (Personal names are not identified as either Arab or Hebrew because some are imported from other languages.)

In *Watch Out for Flying Kids*, geographical names are spelled the way they appear on most maps. Personal names are spelled the way that the people themselves choose to spell them, since they know at least some English.

Note that
- "ah" sounds like the "a" in "father."
- "ch" indicates a guttural sound—like pronouncing the sound of the letter "h" while gargling, not as in "chew."
- "gh" is a hard "g," as in "go," rather than soft, as in "gee."

The Lower Galilee

Personal Names

Ahmad Sanallah	ACH-mahd	SAH-nah-lah
Ahmed Asadi	ACH-med	AH-sah-de
Ali Hasarme	AH-lee	hah-SAR-may
Amit Gelman	ah-MEET	GHEL-mahn
Aya Aa'mar	ah-yah	ah-MER
Dagan Dishbak	dah-GAHN	DEESH-bahk
Dana Raz	DAH-na	RAHZ
Einat Opalin	ay-NOT	oh-pah-LEEN
Fatmi Ali	FAHT-me	AH-lee
Gilad Finkel	gheel-AHD	FEEN-kle
Hala Asadi	CHAH-lah	AH-sah-dee
Hanni Podlipsky	CHAH-nee	pod-LEEP-skee
Hanoch Shafran	hah-NOCH	shah-FRAHN
Hla Asadi	HAH-lah	AH-sah-dee
Leonid Tzipkis	lay-oh-NEED	TZEEP-kees
Manal Asadi	mah-NAHL	AH-sah-dee
Manar Asadi	mah-NAR	AH-sah-dee
Mysa Kabat	MY-suh	KAH-baht
Noam Davidovich	NO-ahm	dah-VEED-o-veetch
Roey Shafran	roe-EE	shah-FRAHN
Saeed Assaf	sah-EED	ah-SAHF
Saher Sanallah	SAH-her	SAH-nah-lah
Salam Abu Zeid	sah-LAHM	AH-boo Zade
Samer Sanallah	SAH-mare	SAH-nah-lah
Shai Ben Yosef	SHY	ben YO-sef
Shirel Mondrik	shee-REL	MON-dreek
Tamer Sanallah	TAH-mare	SAH-nah-lah
Yaron Davidovich	yah-RONE	dah-VEED-o-veetch

Place Names

Al-Aqsa (A)	ahl AHK-sah
Atzmon (H)	ahts-MONE
Bet Kessler (H)	bate KESS-lehr
Biane (A)	beh-AY-neh
Deir al-Asad (A)	DARE ahl AH-sahd
Galil (H)	gah-LEEL
Golan (H)	go-LAHN
Hilazon (H)	hee-lah-ZONE
Karmiel (H)	car-mee-EL
Majd al-Krum (A)	MAjd ahl-KROOM
Misgav (H)	mees-GAHV
Negev (H)	NEH-gev
Sasa (H)	SAH-SAH
Sha'ab (A)	SHAH-AHB
Shorashim (H)	shore-ah-SHEEM

Words and Expressions

Bageli (H)	BAY-geh-leh
Bar Mitzvah (H)	bar MITZ-vah
Bat Mitzvah (H)	baht MITZ-vah
Eid al-Fitr (A)	EED ahl-FEE-ter
Fajr (A)	FAH-jer
Falafel (A/H)	fah-LAH-fell
Hamas (A)	chah-MAHS
Hezbollah (A)	hez-BAHL-LLAH
Hummus (A/H)	CHOO-moose
Hijab (A)	hee-JAHB
Iftar (A)	IF-tar
Intifada (A)	IN-tih-FAH-dah
Jilbab (A)	jeel-BAHB
Kibbeh (A)	KIB-beh
Kibbutz (H)	key-BOOTZ (as in "look")
Kirkas (H)	keer-KAHS

Ma'assalama (A)	mah-AH AHS-sah-lah-MAH
Matkot (H)	maht-KOTE
Mazel tov (H)	mah-ZAHL tove
Mishma'at (H)	meesh-MAH-aht
Nakba (A)	NAHK-bah
Pita (H)	PEE-tah
Qur'an (A)	kur-AHN
Ramadan (A)	RAH-MAH-DAHN
Rosh Hashanah (H)	ROSHE hah-shah-NAH
Sababa (A/H)	sah-BAH-bah
Salaam (A)	sah-LAHM
Serk (A)	SERK
Shalom (H)	shah-LOME
Shemini Atzeret (H)	sh-ME-nee ah-TSAIR-et
Shishlik (A/H)	shee-SHLEEK
Shuk (H)	SHOOK (*as in "loose"*)
Simchat Torah (H)	seem-CHAHT toe-RAH
Sovivich (H)	so-vee-VEECH
Sukkot (H)	soo-KOTE
Tallit (H)	tah-LEET
Tefillin (H)	t-fee-LEEN
Tisha B'av (H)	teesh-AH beh-AHV
Torah (H)	toe-RAH
Tzedakah (H)	tsuh-DAH-kah
Tzehu le Shalom (H)	tsoo luh shah-LOME
Yom Ha'atzmaut (H)	yome ha-AHTZ-mah-OOT
Yom Kippur (H)	yome KEE-poor
Za'atar (A/H)	ZAH-ah-tar
Zhug (A/H)	z'chug

> *"[Circus is] a compulsion to like to do crazy things, to push the boundaries of what is humanly possible."*
>
> —Laura Ricci

A decorative dragon stands guard at City Museum

Circus is a big tent.

That doesn't mean that circuses always perform in tents. But wherever circuses perform, they encompass worlds:

~ a world of tricks, from pratfalls to flying
~ a world of sounds, from lilting to blaring
~ a world of costumes, from dainty to glitzy
~ a world of feelings, from fun to fear and back again
~ a world of troupers, from around the globe
~ a world so thoroughly entrancing that circus creates its own universe.

The Universe of Circus

What comes to mind when you think of a circus? Clowns? Wire-walkers, elephants, human cannonballs, cotton candy? All of these—and more—can fit. Circuses have changed over time, and they display different styles in different places. Performers generally agree on these five common elements:

• Acrobatics, including contortion, mini-trampoline, Pyramid, and tumbling (solo movements like flipping and springing)
• Aerials, including tightwire, lyra, silks, and flying and static trapeze
• Equilibristics (balancing), including rolling globe, rolla bolla, and unicycle

- Object manipulation, including juggling, diabolo, poi, and staff twirling
- Clowning

Some pros also include animal acts.

The World of Youth Circus

Watch Out for Flying Kids spotlights a little-known corner of this universe: youth social circus.

As the first word of the name suggests, "youth circus" refers to programs in which the performers are children. The nine performers featured in this book are teenagers.

The word "social" refers to the mission of bringing together young people who would not ordinarily meet—or, if they did, might fear or oppose each other. The two organizations portrayed in this book—the St. Louis Arches and the Galilee Circus—bring together young people from vastly different backgrounds and cultures through training in circus arts. The goal of both groups is to replace fear with respect and opposition with trust, changing the world one acrobat, contortionist, and flyer at a time.

Why wouldn't these kids meet if it weren't for circus? Why might they even fear or mistrust one another? The three white and two black troupers who are Arches live in different neighborhoods and go to different schools in St. Louis, Missouri, a city that is segregated by race and income level. The two Arabs and two Jews who perform with the Galilee Circus in northern Israel live in towns segregated by religion, ethnicity, language, and history. They represent groups that have been violently at odds with each other for hundreds of years.

Watch Out for Flying Kids shows what happens when all of them get together. That is, it demonstrates how they learn to juggle their responsibilities, fly above the fray, balance schoolwork and circus work, unicycle circles around people who doubt them, tumble gracefully through life—even when injured—and walk the tightrope of politics and friendships.

CHAPTER ONE

THE ST. LOUIS ARCHES

"You have to embrace dropping. Dropping is a good thing. It's a sign you're trying something hard and something new."

—Richard Kennison

Of the more than 700 kids who took classes at Circus Harmony in 2012, only ten were skilled enough to be designated a St. Louis Arch.

The five Arches at the center of this book had worked hard to get there. They astounded audiences, and sometimes themselves, with their feats. Through years of practice, failure, and even injuries, they had developed the necessary flexibility, strength, courage, and trust to become part of a unified team.

But each of these individuals came from different circumstances. Some were black, some white. Some came from the upper-class, others from the middle-class or the under-class. Some lived within stable families while others grew up in splintered families. Each Arch grew up in a different neighborhood of metropolitan, midwestern St. Louis, Missouri, and attended different kinds of schools. As a result, each one found circus in a different way.

Second Most Dangerous

Named for King Louis IX of France, St. Louis was founded in 1764 as a fur-trading post. A century later, the frontier town was so prominent that some people suggested making it the capital of the United States.

The St. Louis skyline

With the growth of railroads in the nineteenth century, St. Louis became known as the Gateway to the West. In 1904, the city, which was then the fourth largest in America, hosted both the Olympic Games and the largest-ever World's Fair up to that date.

With the exception of the often-successful St. Louis Cardinals baseball team, the early twentieth century may have been the high point for St. Louis. Beginning in the 1920s, wealthy people fled to the suburbs as black people from the Deep South moved to the city looking for jobs. In 1876, the city of St. Louis had voted to separate itself from St. Louis County, so these suburbs consisted of separate municipalities or counties, each with its own mostly white schools and superior services.

Segregation laws and customs prevented blacks from moving to the suburbs, and much of the inner city began to turn into slums. Many businesses that remained in the downtown area, such as stores and restaurants, refused to serve black customers. When the mayor ordered a public park desegregated in 1949, whites retaliated by beating blacks, and riots ensued.

Urban renewal projects in the 1960s built highways across St. Louis, slashing apart neighborhoods and forcing even more residents, who were generally black and poor, into public housing and tenements. The remaining blacks who could afford to escaped to nearby suburbs on the north side of the city, and whites moved even farther out.

In some of the increasingly black neighborhoods, the political leadership remained in the control of white people. Black residents felt that city councils, school boards, and police discriminated against them.

Various school desegregation programs, begun in 1980, allowed students to transfer between the city of St. Louis and outlying county schools. These programs reduced racial separation somewhat. But the plans have not been stable, and urban schools remained underfunded and under-performing.

The 1965 construction of the St. Louis Arch, the tallest man-made monument in the world, and other rehab projects have

5

brought tourists and trade back into town. Still, in 2013, the city, with a population of about 318,000 and falling, ranked as the second most dangerous in the country; it had the third-highest murder rate. The greater metropolitan area, with a population approaching three million, is on average far safer.

Racial, educational, economic, and other distinctions between the inner city and the suburbs have persisted. These distinctions define the very different backgrounds of the Arches.

Kellin Quinn Hentoff-Killian

Kellin Quinn Hentoff-Killian, age 6

As soon as his mother disappeared into her office, Kellin toddled over to the case of juggling equipment and pulled himself onto his tiptoes. The two-year-old reached up and grabbed a ball in one hand, then another in his other hand. He placed them carefully on the floor and did the same with another pair of balls. Then he pretended to juggle.

Kellin knew what to do—sort of—because he'd been watching older kids juggle nearly every day since he was an infant. He had been with his mother, Jessica Hentoff, when she negotiated with Bob Cassilly, the eccentric owner and designer of City Museum, for space to house Circus Harmony, where she was the artistic and executive director. Kellin had watched his older siblings learn to walk on globes. Born into and growing up within the circus, he could ride a unicycle before he could handle a bike.

After Circus Harmony moved into its new home at City Museum, Kellin and his family seemed to spend more time there than at home. "We were at the circus a lot, when they were little," Jessica said. "It was really not good how much we were at the circus."

Kellin could explore City Museum 24/7 because he didn't go to school, at least, not in a traditional school building. Jessica homeschooled him and his siblings, Elliana and Keaton. Kellin did his math and English worksheets in an unusual place. "We had a circus train," he said, "with three big circus train cages. There were giant stuffed animals, like tigers. I would squeeze through the bars and do my work there."

Mostly, though, Kellin juggled. "I concentrate on my juggling," he said. "I'm not good at concentrating on school."

One day, when he was six, Kellin announced, "I want to be in the one o'clock show tomorrow."

"Doing what?" his mother asked.

"I made an act."

And he had. While Jessica was working, Kellin had planned and choreographed a fifteen-minute juggling routine, with a beginning, middle, and end. Many novice jugglers' presentations are very simple and don't last longer than a minute. Even veteran performers' acts conclude within about ten minutes. But Kellin's routine progressed from handling ordinary items, like balls, to more challenging objects, like clubs, and from basic cascade patterns to more complex maneuvers.

The next day, he played the one o'clock show. He even "styled"—stood up straight, flung his arms out, and grinned—after every trick. The audience was transfixed.

From then on, Kellin performed regularly with the Arches. His mother paid him, just as she did the older troupers, for appearing in Circus Harmony's multiple weekly shows at the Museum. Like the veterans, he even passed the bucket after each show to collect donations to help cover their salaries, coaching, and costumes.

Jessica usually doesn't teach juggling to children younger than eleven because, in her experience, their eye-hand coordination isn't good enough. A complicated maneuver like juggling would be too frustrating for most young kids. But when Kellin was seven or eight years old, Richard Kennison joined the Circus Harmony team as a juggling coach. He started giving Kellin private lessons. "Kellin did learn early," Richard agreed.

However, Kellin had to work hard like everybody else. "He had to pick up balls and try and fail. Try again and fail. Failure is part of the process to success," Richard explained. "You have to embrace dropping. Dropping is a good thing. It's a sign you're trying something hard and something new."

City Museum

City Museum's 600,000-square foot building began life as the International Shoe Company. A local artist named Bob Cassilly bought the empty structure in 1983 and opened it to the amazed public in 1997. Its ever-changing zany features include a ten-story slide (converted from the chutes through which workers sent shoes to different levels in the factory); a school bus, the front half of which hangs, on hydraulic suspension, off the side of the building and bounces up and down when visitors jump inside it; Daniel Boone's log cabin; The World Aquarium, which is also an animal rehabilitation center and contains a crawl-through shark tank; a thirty-foot high Ferris wheel—and Circus Harmony.

Kellin kept trying, all right.

"We would go to the grocery store," Elliana recalled, "and he would juggle the fruits and vegetables! If he thinks he can juggle it, it's going to happen."

Kellin advanced from handling three balls to four. Within months, even four balls weren't enough to satisfy him.

He demanded knives—and not just the cheap, dull blades Circus Harmony already owned, but attractive, expensive, sharp knives. His mother refused to buy them, so Kellin entered a local juggling competition. Even though many of the other contestants were professionals, Kellin won. He used his $300 prize to buy his own professional juggling knives—real metal rather than plastic.

Sidney Akeem ("Iking") Bateman

"Could we leave?" eleven-year-old Iking pleaded with his mentor, Diane. The circus was only halfway over and he was ready to go.

Iking was the sixth of eight children, all of whom were being raised in a two-bedroom, shingle bungalow by their grandmother. His mother had died in prison when he was three, and he'd never met his father.

Iking had been identified as "high risk" by his school. An organization called Discovering Options, which finds mentors for kids likely to drop out of school, arranged for him to meet once a week with Diane Rankin, a white woman who happened to be a psychiatrist and psychoanalyst. The arrangement was only supposed to last for three months. At first, Iking was too shy to talk with Diane; she suspected he wanted to "fire" her. But ten months later, she was still taking him to McDonald's, reading to him, and searching for other activities he might enjoy.

Iking told Diane that a couple of his brothers had taught him how to tumble on the mattresses spread across the floor of their bedroom. She had already taken him to a gym where he had demonstrated midair backward somersaults. In July 2003, she took him to see Circus Flora, a professional troupe. It featured an elephant, clowns, jugglers, and wire walkers—and the St. Louis

Iking Bateman, age 12

Arches, who dazzled the audience with their power tumbling.

Diane had arranged for Iking to meet Jessica at intermission. She knew that Circus Harmony welcomed talented tumblers, especially those who could benefit both from the family atmosphere and from the structure that the program offered—elements that were missing from Iking's life.

Iking and Diane watched the first half of the show. But at intermission he asked to leave. He didn't even want to wait around to see the Arches or meet Jessica.

"Are you sure you don't want to stay?" Diane asked.

"Yes," he insisted. "It's not interesting to me."

I can't pick him up and carry him backstage, she reasoned. So, they left.

Diane Rankin

Throughout the fall of 2003, Diane took Iking on weekend excursions—but she had to pick him up and drop him off at his grandmother's during daylight. "My neighborhood is really bad," Iking said. "It's not a neighborhood you'd go outside and sit outside on your front porch and, like, relax and chill. You'd be afraid of guns shooting in the next street, high-speed chases, stolen cars flying down the street.… But, I have to live in it."

Nearly a third of the people who lived in his neighborhood were poor. Almost half had dropped out before graduating from high school. And, like most of St. Louis's inner-city areas north of Delmar Avenue, the informal but real black-white dividing line, it was 97 percent black.

Discovering Options was right in pegging Iking as at-risk. His teachers didn't know how to help or handle him. Sometimes he clowned around, ignoring them. At other times, he got into fistfights. Unlike other people, Diane didn't scream at him. "Okay, Iking, let's think about this," she'd say. "What happens when you fight? Could you do something else, instead?"

She tried to talk with his teacher or principal but they rarely had time to discuss Iking. His home life was too disorganized for anyone to transfer him to another school. The staff told Diane that Iking needed a black male authority figure in his life.

Do You Want to Be an Arch?

Required skills for the Arches have increased over time. Typical examples include the following:

- Do five pull-ups, five chin-ups, and fifteen push-ups
- Hold hand stand for twenty seconds
- Do three back handsprings
- Hold a flyer as a base and elevate to a shoulder stand as a flyer
- Tuck and pike from a mini-tramp
- Hula hoop on a rolling globe; step through a hoop on a rolla bolla
- Pop and catch diabolos; juggle and pass three clubs
- Hang by ankles from a trapeze; climb and descend aerial web
- Unicycle
- Choreograph a four-minute act

"He has me," she responded.

Meanwhile, she kept urging him to visit Circus Harmony. Finally, in January 2004, he consented. "I saw some tumbling mats in the circus area," Iking said, "and I ran on them into the ring and started tumbling."

But Donald Hughes stopped him. "You can't be tumbling on the mats," the young black coach told Iking. "Insurance reasons. You have to be one of the students of the school."

"So, right there," Iking said, "I got brochures and papers and signed up for a class."

That's also when he acquired his nickname. At school, everyone called him Sidney. He wanted to use a different name for circus, so he offered Akeem, his middle name. But even that didn't seem exotic enough. So when the office manager asked him how he spelled it, he blurted out, "I-K-I-N-G," and it stuck.

Iking had never had formal training in tumbling; he was what Donald called a street tumbler. He was strong and quick, but his legs cocked at odd angles when he did his tricks, and his toes weren't pointed. Donald worked with Iking on straightening his legs, pointing his toes, and using momentum rather than sheer muscle power to propel himself.

"At the beginning, he was stubborn because he felt that he knew a lot," Donald said. "He thought it [his skill] was better than what it was." Fortunately, Iking was willing to learn. "He had a great attitude. He always wanted to get better."

Iking improved quickly, and at the end of the first ten-week session of classes Jessica asked him if he'd like to join the advanced group, the Arches. (In those days, the entrance requirements were informal, so it wasn't unusual for a young performer who didn't yet juggle or unicycle to join.) He didn't know what the Arches were expected to do but agreed he'd give it a try.

"I was shy. I wasn't quite sure about it," Iking said. "But they accepted me really quickly." Not only did the kids welcome him, but the activities were fun too. "I was, like, I could probably get used to this." As an Arch, he could be in Circus Flora that year.

And then he broke his foot.

"We was carrying the mini-trampoline out of the ring after practice, and I tripped over a speed bump. I fell, and the crash pad fell on my foot. It was bad."

Iking appeared in the official Arches-at-Flora photograph as a member of the troupe, but he couldn't perform.

Meghan Clark

Meghan strolled through Laumeier Sculpture Park with her parents and younger brother. The Clarks noticed a crowd gathering nearby, so they joined it and sat down on the grass.

Even though the Clarks had moved to the outer suburbs of St. Louis six months earlier, Meghan still didn't feel settled. She didn't have many friends in fifth grade and she didn't know what sports she wanted to play.

Things were different in St. Louis. "We had maybe three black people in my entire school in Green Bay," she said. "On my first day of school in St. Louis, there were like ten or twelve [black] students in my classroom alone."

She noted other differences. In Wisconsin, she recalled, "you're either Catholic or you're Lutheran, and many people know you along those lines." But in St. Louis, "every religion has a temple or a shrine or a church on this one street that's in the district for our school. We get a lot of diverse students."

Because her elementary school in Green Bay had been pretty homogeneous, almost everyone hung out together. In her new middle school, however, she noticed that kids formed groups based on color or religion or income. "I thought it was weird.... There was a lot of separation between the blacks and the whites and the Muslims.... People separated along class lines as well."

Sitting in the park, Meghan watched a group of kids who were tumbling and performing acrobatics. "It was kids my age," she said, "doing something cool." As she observed these preteens,

Meghan Clark, age 12, on the right, Donesha Buhr on the left

11

she recognized some of the skills she had learned in dance and gymnastics, but she knew there was a big difference.

"I knew how to do some of it and definitely thought I could learn. At the same time, I was in awe," she said. These kids were so polished, Meghan noticed. "They were able to get applause from people other than people related to them!"

The performers turned out to be the Arches. It was a diverse group of kids, like those at her school, but they weren't segregating themselves. They were clambering over each other and supporting one another. Even before the performance ended, Meghan told her parents she wanted to take circus classes.

"It seemed attainable but I'd have to work for it, which I like," she said.

She started in the fall of 2006, when she entered seventh grade. "I showed up to my first class, and I had to be in the beginning class," Meghan said. "I was a little annoyed about that because there were much younger kids than I was." She was already proficient in many of the skills the beginners were just learning. "Forward and backward rolls, round-offs, front and back walkovers—that's what I'd just do on the playground for fun."

Meghan's father asked Jessica if she could be moved up to the intermediate class. Jessica watched Meghan go through her paces and said, "Hey, she is kind of flexible." She promoted her after the first semester. Even though Meghan felt intimidated because the other students were more advanced, she liked being with kids her own age.

"I like looking up to people," she said, "rather than feeling superior."

Shaina Hughes

Shaina made her circus debut when she was only eight months old. She stood in her father's hand while he strolled, atop a large rubber globe, into Circus Harmony's ring. She doesn't remember the trick, of course, but she's seen the pictures of her dad, Donald Hughes, balancing her "like a feather."

By the time Shaina was four years old, her father began formally coaching her. "I started tumbling," Shaina said, "learning how to do cartwheels and the basics, like forward rolls and plate-spinning…. I'm a fast learner, and I learned how to do everything."

Because Shaina was so adept, Jessica made her an Arch and started paying her to perform in Circus Harmony's regular shows. During her dad's act, Shaina waited, as quietly as an excitable five-year-old could, until the music changed. Then she dashed into the ring, where her dad swept her up and planted her feet on his shoulders. Shaina balanced and styled like a pro.

The following year, she and her father worked on a trick they called The Thinker, after the bronze statue by Auguste Rodin. She posed with her chin in her hand, while balanced in a one-legged squat on her father's shoulder and wrist.

"It was really hard at first," Shaina said, "and really scary… because he wasn't holding on, and I didn't have anything to hold onto."

Once she stopped swaying and found her balance, she felt proud. But her father wasn't satisfied. He wanted them to make the trick even riskier by performing it while he tried to keep his balance on a rolling globe.

"I didn't want to do it at first," Shaina said. "I was afraid I was going to fall. But…my dad reassured me that I wasn't going to fall and that [if I did] someone would catch me."

While her dad shifted his feet back and forth on the globe so that he didn't roll right off, Shaina cautiously maneuvered herself into position.

"After the first time I did it," she said, "it was okay. I wasn't scared after that."

For her finale, Shaina did a forward roll from her father's shoulder onto the globe on which he stood. "The audience thought it was amazing!"

At that age, she loved everything about circus—from her costume to the audience's clapping. As she grew older, though,

Donald Hughes was one of Jessica's first students. He believed that circus had kept him off the streets and out of jail—maybe even saved his life. "Most of the times my [old] friends were hanging out on the corner, I was at somebody's gym practicing…. Most of [them] are either in jail or dead…. I'm still alive."

Shaina was born when Donald was nineteen. Fearing that his daughter might face the same dangers and temptations he had, he enrolled her in circus classes as soon as possible.

13

*Shaina Hughes, age 5,
and Elliana Hentoff-Killian, age 7*

she didn't always think it was amazing to live with her coach. Her parents split up when she was about three, and she divided her time among her mom's, her dad's, and her grandmother's places. She and her mother moved frequently. By the time Shaina was eleven years old, she'd lived in about ten different homes and attended multiple elementary schools. She spent every summer with her dad because he could ferry her to circus, where he still worked. But at times, she wasn't sure she wanted to go anymore.

"It was pretty hard because, even when we were not at circus, when we were at home, I'd still have to practice, and I'd still get critiqued. He would tell me what I need to work on and what I'm doing really well. It was like having a full-time coach. At first, I didn't take it so well because I felt like my dad was always targeting me." Several times she became so frustrated that she nearly quit circus.

Around the time they were practicing The Thinker, Shaina told her dad she wanted to get her back handspring. "I was working really hard every day. I just couldn't get it," she said. "I was really upset."

"Keep practicing," her father insisted. After all, mastering her back handspring had been her idea, not his. And, once she set a goal, he was going to make sure she met it.

After trying and failing time after time, she finally yelled, "I never will be able to get this. I don't ever want to do this again!"

"Keep trying."

"I don't want to do it. I give up."

"You will get it," he assured her.

At that point she was sure that she would not. Furthermore, she didn't care. Then, one day when her father was out of town, her mood shifted.

"Something told me that day to trust my instincts and go for it. When I did it that one more time, I got my back handspring!"

When her father returned to town, she was excited to show him that she could do it on her own. Initially, she was nervous because he was watching her, and she missed.

This time she assured him, "No, wait. I can get this." And she did—from then on. Back handsprings were exhilarating. "When I go fast, it looks like arches going across the ground.... It's like colors flying past.... When you're in a room full of colors, it's very beautiful."

15

All of the practices paid off. By the time she was seven, she could tumble, juggle three balls, and perform a fast-spinning act on the lyra, a circular trapeze.

The Arches became a way of life and a family. Donavon and Lil Donald, her two younger half-brothers, also performed in the circus. They sometimes put on shows together for her friends' birthday parties.

Just before her eleventh birthday, everything changed. Shaina was spending the night at Jessica's house. She and other kids stayed there often enough that Jessica kept a rack that held twenty-five toothbrushes on her bathroom wall, each space labeled with a child's name.

The next morning, Shaina's mother picked her up. "We're moving to a town in Illinois called Rock Island," she announced. She didn't give an explanation, but Shaina worked out that her mother's newest boyfriend lived there.

"I didn't want to go," Shaina said. But she had no alternative. She couldn't stay with her father. He didn't have custody. Jessica invited her to move in but Shaina's mother refused. Within days, Shaina, her mother, and her younger half-sister moved to Illinois.

Alexandra Gabliani

Alex stared at the floor lamp in the living room while her adoptive mother talked on the telephone. Recently arrived in St. Louis from an orphanage in Russia, Alex had discovered lots of spaces to explore in her new home and neighborhood. Directly across the street lay Oak Knoll Park, a rambling, wooded expanse with picnic tables, trails, a pond, and a playground.

But at that moment, two-year-old Alex was bored, waiting for her mother to get off the phone. The long pole on the lamp intrigued her. Surely, she figured, she could climb up and reach whatever was at the top. So she gave it a try.

Her mother "freaked out," Alex said, and exclaimed, "We need to do something with you!"

Not long after that, her parents enrolled Alex in gymnastics class. Initially she learned basic skills, like forward and backward rolls and walkovers, as well as hanging and swinging from a bar. Beginning when she was six, Alex attended a circus day camp during the summer. The program was run by Alexandre ("Sacha") Pavlata, who had taught the first group of Arches with Jessica. Alex learned partner acrobatics, trampoline, and some juggling.

"Lots of kids from my school went," she said. "It was just one of those popular things that every kid wants to be a part of."

Between gymnastics during the school year and circus camp over the summer, Alex grew strong and flexible. By the time she was eight years old, she could handle front and back handsprings and was learning to do back tucks. In fact, her tumbling and acrobatic skills were strong enough that she began to participate in competitions. But she found them unappealing.

"I didn't like working so many hours just to compete with my friends," Alex said. "It took the fun out of the sport.… Suddenly, we weren't very friendly with each other because we were trying to do better than each other." Also, the routines were structured and mandated. She preferred more open-ended, freewheeling activities.

The camp moved to a large gymnasium, where Sacha set up aerial equipment including flying trapeze, cradle, and cloud swing. Because Alex had developed more flexibility and strength in gymnastics than other kids her age, he worked with her on skills that the others weren't ready for yet.

"I've always liked powerful acts that require constant movement," Alex said. "So, I liked swinging." She'd wrap her legs around the ropes of the cloud swing, pump with her knees, lean forward—and let go.

Best of all was flying trapeze. "I was too small to reach the bar on my own," she recalled. "So the person who held me literally picked me up and helped me grab the bar."

Fortunately, her hands were already callused from her many hours doing gymnastics. The trapeze bar, a length of thick metal

The St. Louis Arches at Circus Harmony in 2005 From left: Junior Williams, Matt Viverito, Iking, Elliana, Casey Tkaz, Lemond Carmickle, Alex Gabliani, Shaina, Keaton Hentoff-Killian, Kellin, Lil Donald Hughes

wrapped in tape, can scrape and blister children's hands. But Alex didn't notice the pain.

"I reached out my hands while she held onto my waist. She would give me a push, let go, and I would swing... Flying felt very free... It's a feeling you can't get from anything else—the freedom and the power that you feel while you're swinging. It feels like you're pushing everything else away. Nothing matters other than the swing [and] the bar."

Alex adored the lofty freedom of aerials so much that she became impatient with the strict ground rules of gymnastics. When Sacha announced that he planned to move to Boston to open a circus school, he asked Alex's parents if she could move with him.

Alex realized that wasn't possible. Still, she told Sacha, "I want to run away and join the circus."

"I'll help you," he told her. He took Alex across town to meet his friend Jessica at Circus Harmony.

"It was chaos," Alex recalled gleefully. Tumbling mats and circus props were scattered around, and lots of kids were bouncing and socializing. Jessica auditioned Alex and immediately named her an Arch. Alex wasn't a bit sorry that she'd quit gymnastics. Now she could do circus year-round!

Many of her new teammates didn't live in the western suburbs, as she did. Sometimes when her nanny picked her up after practice, she gave kids rides and dropped them off at their homes downtown. "My friends' houses were so much smaller and so much more broken down than mine," Alex noticed. A few of these kids called her "the rich girl," which upset and confused her.

Just months later, Alex participated in her first circus show—so different from gymnastics competitions. Even though she found the costumes ugly, the show was thrilling. The Arches performed before a St. Louis Rams football game. She walked on a globe, did a tumbling routine, and handed Keaton his juggling props. The audience loved the youthful circus troupers. And Alex loved the crowd, the freedom, and the lack of competition.

Jessica Hentoff and the St. Louis Arches

It's not unusual for college students to set off a dormitory fire alarm as a prank. But Jessica set hers off by accident—while practicing fire-eating.

As a bookish child from New York City, Jessica didn't climb a tree until she was ten years old. In college she needed to find a class that fit her schedule and chose one called Circus. She learned to juggle, clown, tumble, unicycle, and walk on stilts. Enthralled by pushing her body to its limits, she became known at school as "that circus girl."

*Jessica Hentoff holds
her son Keaton, age 1*

Her parents were amused by her hobby until she tried fire-eating. Jessica and her father, Nat Hentoff—a prominent writer, political activist, and music critic—had a face-off. He "thunderously disapproved" of her pyrotechnics. Instead of giving up fire-eating, she added aerials to her repertoire, which he did not consider an improvement. But after her teacher Warren Bacon taught her how to fly, Jessica never looked down—or back.

Desperate to expand her skills, she wrote to fifty circuses, searching for a summer job after her freshman year. "I'll do anything," she pleaded. "I'll water the elephants. I'll clean up after them. Anything at all."

The only one that responded was a Methodist youth circus named The Circus Kingdom. Because she was Jewish, Jessica wondered if they'd made a mistake. But the director, Reverend David Harris, told her, "This circus is about people from all backgrounds."

The circus's performers—mostly high school and college students—put on shows in retirement homes, prisons, and youth facilities. That summer, Jessica learned that circus wasn't only about juggling and tumbling. It was really about "the brotherhood of man and how we can all get along."

She told Warren, "This is what I want to do with my life." He didn't think Jessica was a particularly gifted circus performer, but he knew she was willing to work hard. He agreed to help.

When Jessica graduated from college, she heard about a new kind of circus that was starting up in New York City. Big Apple Circus promised to be different from traditional, three-ring American circuses. It was nonprofit and all the action was staged in one ring. Sensing that "there is magic in that one ring," she called Warren.

"You've got to come to New York," she told him. "This is the renaissance of American circus."

Warren and Jessica became partners and did aerials with Big Apple for two years, while Jessica also performed acrobatics with another partner. After that, she and Warren went out on the road with the Coronas Aerial Thrill Circus.

Things were going well...until the day Jessica fell.

They were doing an aerials perch act in Kansas City, Missouri, in 1979. Two clowns were spotting them to make sure they didn't land on their heads or backs if they fell. The clowns, however, got distracted at the exact moment that Jessica was supposed to catch the trapeze rope with her foot. But she didn't.

She fell thirty feet, dislocating her shoulder and gashing her leg. At that moment, Jessica realized that circus was truly dangerous. She debated quitting. During the several months that it took her to heal, she repeatedly asked herself, "Do you really want to do this?" She concluded that she did.

Jessica and her father quarreled bitterly over her decision.

"Living in New York is much more dangerous," she argued.

"The odds are alarmingly different when you spend your working hours where only birds are naturally at home," he retorted. Jessica's father was so infuriated that he refused to speak to her.

When she was about eleven years old, she had told him, "I want my name to be known." Now, she determined, "If I was going to go back, I was going to do something exceptional." She intended to concoct an act that no other performer had ever accomplished.

To develop her new routine, she knew she needed to attend professional circus school. At the Circus Arts Center in New Jersey, Jessica studied with two of the world's top coaches from the famously demanding Moscow Circus School. There, she met Kathie Hoyer, who eventually became her new aerials partner. Together they developed a double-trapeze trick called Heel-to-Heel that no one had ever done before or has ever repeated.

In 1985, the two women moved to St. Louis. Kathie had grown up there, and the town was centrally located for their forays around the country. Circus Flora hired them and, not long afterward, established its headquarters in St. Louis.

The following year, Nat watched his daughter perform for the first time. In an article in the *Wall Street Journal,* he wrote that

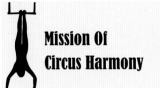

Mission Of Circus Harmony

"Circus Harmony teaches the art of life through circus education. We work to build character and expand community for youth of all ages, cultures, abilities and backgrounds. Through teaching and performance of circus arts, we help people defy gravity, soar with confidence, and leap over social barriers, all at the same time."

until then, he had "refused to attend any of Jessica's performances for two reasons—protest and fear." As she climbed a rope to near the top of Flora's tent, he grew fearful for her.

"But once the act began," he continued, "I became so involved in the unfolding of its choreography that I forgot to be afraid."

Jessica felt that her father's article was, finally, "his ultimate form of acceptance." After five years, they could talk to one another again.

Three years later, David Balding—the founder, artistic director, and producer of Circus Flora—asked Jessica to start a youth program. She recalled something that Warren had told her when she thanked him for introducing her to circus in college: "Pass it on."

It was time to do that.

Jessica created the St. Louis Arches, named for the city's soaring steel monument on the Mississippi River and for her students' graceful back bends. Six or seven years later, Bob agreed to provide space at City Museum, rent-free. In exchange, Jessica promised to present circus shows to the museum's visitors, cost-free.

After a decade, Flora withdrew its financial support for the youth program; David decided to focus on performing rather than teaching children. But Jessica knew she couldn't quit. After all, second-generation students like Shaina needed circus too. So in 2001, she established Circus Harmony as an independent, nonprofit social circus for children, with the St. Louis Arches as the new company's performance troupe.

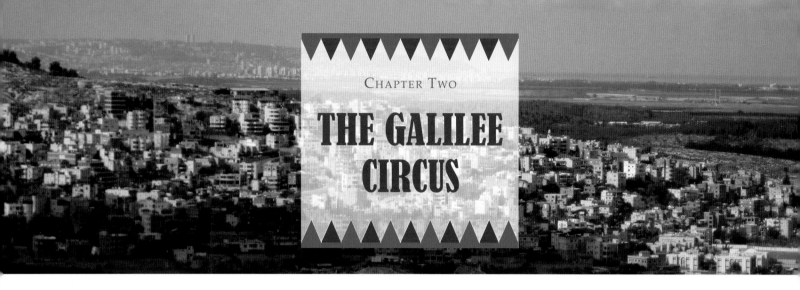

CHAPTER TWO

THE GALILEE CIRCUS

The fifty or so students in the Galilee Circus lived in several villages in the mountainous northern region of Israel that is called the Galilee. Just as Iking and Shaina grew up in "black" neighborhoods and Meghan and Alex in "white" ones, the Israeli circus kids were from villages that were either all Arab or almost all Jewish. As a result, the four Galilee troupers converged on circus from different starting points.

Independence or Catastrophe?

Israel is shaped like a fat splinter. In square miles, the entire country covers less territory than the area that encompasses the cities and suburbs of metropolitan St. Louis. You could drive the length of the country—290 miles—in about nine hours. At its narrowest point, it is only seventy-one miles wide. The circus kids' homes lie within ten miles of each other—half of the distance between Iking's and Meghan's neighborhoods.

But despite the compactness of their country, Arab and Jewish children are segregated from each other in multiple ways. Unlike sprawling St. Louis, which merges the inner city, suburbs, and outlying areas into one interconnected metropolitan area, the Galilee's villages are detached from one another. Public bus service among them is irregular, infrequent, and inconvenient.

"Circus is based on trust and overcoming fear and on making people laugh. Those are all in short supply in this part of the world."

—Marc Rosenstein

Sha'ab, an Arab village, as seen from Shorashim, the Jewish town where Marc Rosenstein lives

What's an Arab?
What's a Jew?

Arabs are considered members of an ethnic group that is descended from tribal ancestors who lived around the Arabian Peninsula. Many, though not all, speak Arabic. They can be Christian, Muslim, or Druze.

Jews are considered members of an ethnic group that also shares a common religious heritage. They are descended from tribal ancestors who lived in the Middle East. They speak different languages, though Hebrew is the language of prayer.

As with all groups of people, there are internal differences of opinions and beliefs within both Arab and Jewish populations.

Each village is bounded by laws or security fences and is separated from the next one by rolling hills and olive groves.

The deepest gulf between the Jews and Arabs in the Galilee Circus is not geographical, though. It's cultural. Young people here grow up speaking different languages, each with its own alphabet; the Jewish kids speak Hebrew and the Arab kids Arabic. They practice different religions, absorb different customs, and study somewhat different histories of their tiny, reluctantly shared homeland.

The gulf began over a century earlier with the birth of the Zionist movement in the 1880s. Jewish Zionists fled pogroms (violent attacks) and other forms of anti-Semitism in Eastern Europe. They bought land and settled in what was then called Palestine, where they hoped to establish a new country for Jews in the region that they saw as their Biblical homeland.

At the end of the nineteenth century, nearly 95 percent of the people in Palestine were Arabs. They had been tilling the land and herding sheep for hundreds of years. The land was theirs they believed, and they objected to the intruders from Europe. They demanded that their rulers—first, the Ottoman Turks and then, after the First World War, the British—ban Jewish immigrants. This tactic did not succeed, however. The Jews kept coming.

In 1920, some Arabs in the Galilee started attacking Jewish settlers. Over the next twenty years, the anti-Zionist attacks spread and the violence worsened.

The situation reached a crisis during and after the Second World War. Even more Jews, many of them refugees from the Nazis, came ashore. Fearing the growing tension between the two groups, the British agreed to halt the immigration. They refused entry to many Jewish refugees.

To resolve the issues of where Jews and Arabs could live and how they should be governed, the United Nations proposed dividing Palestine into two countries—one for Arabs and the other for Jews. The Jews accepted this "partition" plan as a way—finally, after 2,000 years—to establish their own state. Arabs rejected the plan, arguing that Jews didn't belong there at all.

On May 15, 1948, the Jews pronounced the portion granted to them an independent country, which they called Israel. The next day, the Arabs declared war on this new state. Jews call this conflict *Milchemet Ha'atzmaut*, the War of Independence. Arabs call these same events the *Nakba*, meaning "the Catastrophe."

The repercussions of these hostilities and subsequent ones continue to rebound, affecting living patterns, social relationships, economic opportunities, and daily life for everyone.

Roey Shafran   רועי שפרן

Roey Shafran, age 10

Roey stared at his friend. Yaron was tossing a cascade of small, brightly colored balls. How did he do that?

"It's easy," Yaron told him. "I could teach you."

With Yaron's help, Roey learned to throw and catch two balls and to roll a diabolo along a string. When Yaron started showing off his tumbling tricks, Roey wanted to know how he'd learned to do those too.

"Circus," Yaron said. He and his older brother had been going to the Galilee Circus for two years, ever since it began. Noam could already juggle five balls.

Kids in the Jewish town of Karmiel, where Roey lived, could choose from lots of after-school programs. "I never thought about circus," Roey said. He had barely even heard of it. But now that he had seen Yaron's skill at juggling, the circus program appealed to him. In the fall of 2005, his mother drove him to the community center for a Galilee Circus open house.

The gymnasium looked gigantic to Roey, who was small for his age. He took it all in, astounded. There were so many kids, and the tricks they were doing with objects, each other, and their own bodies amazed him.

Roey's mother noticed something that he did not: more than half of the kids there were Arab. "I didn't know this was Arabs *and* Jews," she said, delighted to see the kids playing together.

25

Roey's Immigrant Family

Roey is called a sabra—he was born in Israel. But, like many Jewish Israelis, his family converged on the state from other continents. His father's parents were born in Eastern Europe and were preteens when the Nazis sent them to concentration camps. In 1945, at the end of World War II, they arrived in Palestine, as the land was known then, as orphaned refugees. After escaping anti-Semitism in the Ukraine, disease in Egypt, and a dictatorship in Uruguay, Roey's mother and her family came to Israel in 1973.

Many of the Shafrans' Jewish neighbors disapproved of "mixed" activities that tried to promote coexistence between the two groups. Roey's parents, Hanoch and Orly, understood their neighbors' concerns. "Most of them—the Arabs—don't like us," his father said. As a result, some Jews felt afraid of Arabs. Nevertheless, Roey's parents believed, "We have to live with them." They hoped to show that coexistence could work.

After all, about half the residents of the Galilee were Arab—a far higher proportion than in Israel as a whole, where they made up 20 percent of the population. A modern development town, Karmiel drew visitors from the entire region, including Arabs, who shopped in the same stores as Jews when they drove to Karmiel from the nearest villages, Biane, Majd al-Krum, and Deir al-Asad, which were less than three miles away.

The two groups rarely socialized though. At one point, Roey's elementary school joined in a partnership with a school in an Arab village about six miles away. The children visited each other's homes, but they didn't really get to know one other. The arrangement was short-lived. Hanoch had worked closely with Arab colleagues before he retired, and he and Orly visited them on Muslim holy days. But most Jews in serene Karmiel thought it was too dangerous to venture into the congested Arab villages.

Still, some members of the community continued to try to bring Arab and Jewish young people together. Orly and Hanoch hoped that the Galilee Circus would have staying power, that the kids would not only get along but also develop long-term friendships. Connections would be even better than coexistence.

The Shafrans also hoped that Roey would have fun at circus. "He was afraid of a lot of things," Orly said. Roey was fearful of big kids, physical challenges, new situations. Maybe circus would make him braver.

At the beginning of the first class, the circus manager, Ahmad Sanallah, led the group in some ice-breakers. "The manager called everybody," Roey said. "We sat together in a circle. We did all kind of name-games. Everybody says their name. He gave each one a ball, and you'd pass it to someone and say his name."

Though the children couldn't speak each other's language, Ahmad translated for them. This was especially important for the Arab kids because the circus coaches were Jewish and only spoke Hebrew; without Ahmad's help, they wouldn't understand the coaches' directions.

After the name games, they visited stations around the gym, where they tried different circus skills: juggling, flower sticks, poi, staff twirling, and acrobatics. "At each station, the coach did another game to make everybody know each other," Roey recalled. At the flower sticks station, for instance, each child made up a routine for the others to follow. Roey was proud that his moves were the most challenging for everyone.

"I just came to try once," Roey said. But he was hooked. He told his parents he wanted to keep going. They were glad he'd found an activity he enjoyed, especially one that involved both Arabs and Jews.

"The first few months in the circus," Roey said, "I really liked juggling." In fact, he liked it so much, especially diabolo, that he didn't try anything else. Fortunately, he was persistent at his favorite activity. "He was not good at all in the juggling," Gilad Finkel, one of the coaches, said, "and had many difficulties."

But Roey didn't notice the difficulties any more than he noticed that most of the kids weren't Jewish and didn't speak Hebrew. Circus was fun.

Hala Asadi

حلا اسدي

There were no organized activities or parks or playgrounds in Deir al-Asad, the Muslim Arab village where Hala and her family lived. But every Monday afternoon, her brother Ali climbed on the bus heading for the nearby town of Karmiel to attend something called "circus."

Karmiel seemed to exist in a different world from the one Ali knew. Almost every surface in Deir al-Asad, both horizontal and vertical, is carved from stone. Nameless roads, alleys, paths,

"The circus is a small program with a big idea," **Ahmad Sanallah** said. Ahmad, an Arab from Deir al-Asad, has degrees in Hebrew and education from Haifa University. In addition to his work managing the circus, he also teaches Hebrew at an Arab high school.

Palestinians?
Israeli Arabs?

When the 1948 war ended, most Arabs who had been living in Palestine left the new country of Israel. Some were forced out by the Israel Defense Forces (IDF); others fled. Most sought refuge in the Gaza Strip, which belonged to Egypt, or in the West Bank of the Jordan River, which belonged to Jordan. These refugees and their descendants, including some of Hala's relatives, call themselves Palestinians. Arabs who stayed, including Hala's and Hla's grandparents, became citizens of the new state. They are called Israeli Arabs and have the same legal rights as Jews.

and driveways slant at odd angles from each other, leading circuitously to a maze of tightly packed homes with no street addresses. As the bus drove through Karmiel, Ali could see parks and single-family homes with green lawns.

But Ali didn't care about backyards or neighborhoods. He was most interested in the town's community center where he was learning all sorts of tricks. Pretty soon, he could juggle three balls.

Manar and Manal, Hala's older twin sisters, began going to circus a year or so after Ali started. Then their father, Yousef, started volunteering with the circus, setting up seats and hauling equipment for the end-of-year show.

All this time, Hala wondered, *What does that mean—circus?* Like Roey, she'd never heard of one or seen one. Finally, when she was about seven, she went to a Galilee Circus show. Manar was doing forward rolls. Manal was juggling. Ali was balancing on another boy's knees. Now Hala understood.

"Tumbling, juggling, acrobatics!" she exclaimed. "It was a whole new world to me." She told her parents that she wanted to go to circus too. However, she had one reservation.

"I was a little afraid," she admitted. "There were Jewish [kids] there." Hala had seen Jewish children, but she'd never talked with one. How could she? They spoke different languages.

"I had a feeling inside that they might have stereotyped ideas about the Arabs, especially because we're Arabs in a Jewish country," Hala said. "We are in the minority; they are in the majority."

Although the Asadi family, like the Shafrans, believed in coexistence, Manal was well aware that Arabs and Jews rarely mixed. "Everyone knows the relations aren't good," she said. "Arabs hate Jews. Jews hate Arabs."

But circus was different. Jews and Arabs in the Galilee Circus didn't hate each other, Manal explained. "It's different because everyone who comes to this circus is coming for peace." Hala's other sister Manar even told Hala she liked circus because of

the Jews. "I do things with Jews I wouldn't do before."

Her brother and sisters tried to reassure Hala. They'd be there to watch over her. They had picked up some Hebrew at circus, so they could help her communicate.

Hala wasn't completely convinced. "I was worried about working and practicing with Jews," she admitted. "I had never been in such a project that combines Arabs and Jews because there's never been a combination. We'd never been together. They might think they wouldn't want to work with us."

Despite her concerns, Hala decided to join her siblings when classes started up again in the fall. She tried out juggling and acrobatics right away. Within months, she could do forward and backward rolls, spin poi, and even walk on stilts, as long as a coach held her hand.

Hala Asadi, right, age 13, and her cousin Hla Asadi, age 12

As Hala interacted with Jewish kids, her fears began to recede—but they didn't disappear completely. "In the beginning," she noticed, "there were some—not discrimination—but deep down inside, we did feel something different."

Hala wasn't sure how to express the difference she felt, but Mysa Kabat, another Arab girl in the circus, put it this way: "When we joined the Circus, we weren't unified…. As Arabs and Jews, there's animosity amongst us. The Arabs were on their own…. There is always something that makes us feel like we are not good enough."

Shai Ben Yosef   שי בן יוסף

The summer before Shai started second grade, he and his mother visited the annual fair held by the council of Misgav, the region where Shai's village Atzmon is located. Kids could try out different after-school activities, such as art classes, athletics, and academics.

"A juggling teacher was there," Shai said, "and he taught me a bit of juggling. I just loved it!" Shai also picked up a set of flower sticks and quickly got the hang of it. That juggling coach was Gilad Finkel, and he was so impressed that he asked Shai if he had experience. "I was good at it right away," Shai boasted. "I haven't met many people who can do it right away." Shai signed up for Gilad's course.

Shai Ben Yosef, age 13

When the class called Magic and Juggling started that fall, Shai learned a number of fun tricks. The first half of each ninety-minute weekly session focused on magic. Shai learned how to make a coin disappear and then reappear. During the second half of each class, the ten or fifteen kids practiced the basics of flower sticks, poi, rolla bolla, diabolo, and ball juggling.

Shai had a difficult time learning to spin the two poi in a particular pattern. "The Butterfly—for boys, it's very painful," he said. "The poi usually are spinning either forward or backward but they're not spinning on the same plane. In Butterfly, they are on the same plane. Sometimes, they hit each other, and the first place they hit is the groin! Either the head or the groin, depending on which way you're spinning."

As Shai improved, he added unicycle, staff twirling, tight-wire, and stilts to his routines. "I left magic behind," he said.

After five years, Shai was one of the oldest, biggest, and best performers in the class. In 2006, when he was almost thirteen, he was ready to move on to a higher-level class. "Aside from teaching in Misgav," Gilad told him, "I also teach circus in Karmiel."

"A circus?!" Shai exclaimed. He'd heard of circuses but he'd never seen one. He wanted to register right away. But first Gilad needed to have a talk with him and his parents.

"It's a Jewish-Arab circus," Gilad told them. "Do you have any problems with that?"

Why would that matter? Shai wondered. He had met Arab people before. "They were always nice to me," he said.

Arab kids weren't the problem for Shai. The other Jewish kids were. "I was kind of a nerd," he admitted. "People used to pick on me." At school they sometimes called him names. "They would thump me on the back of my head."

So, Shai asked Gilad, "Are the other Jewish kids mean?"

Gilad seemed surprised by Shai's question. He expected him to be nervous about Arabs, not Jews. Tensions between Arabs and Jews seemed more taut than ever. Gilad needed to know in advance that Shai and his family would agree to get along with everyone.

This was not an issue for the Ben Yosef family.

"My mom is all for coexistence," Shai said. "She's in lots of Jewish-Arab projects."

Doron Ben Yosef liked the idea of the circus too. Shai's father taught a high school course that combined history, geography, and Bible. Shai had recently quit taking drum lessons and seemed directionless and unfocused. Doron was happy that his son wanted to get serious about juggling.

Wary of the other Jewish kids but not worried about the Arabs, Shai went to Karmiel for circus. He was already skilled enough that he immediately joined the advanced group, which practiced three hours a week.

Shai recognized Yaron and Noam Davidovich, who had been in his class in Atzmon for a while. "They were the first ones I talked to," Shai said.

Nevertheless, Shai developed more friendships with Arabs than with Jews, especially with Ahmad's son Tamer and a girl named Fatmi Ali. The three of them performed unicycle together but Shai and Fatmi had trouble idling—remaining stationary without rolling backward and forward or falling over. Fortunately, Fatmi spoke Hebrew, so she and Shai could chat while they practiced.

"There was a really big fan with a cover we leaned on," Shai said. "We were next to each other and worked on idling the entire three hours. We were just doing that, and we bonded."

Gilad hoped that Shai could fix his relationships too. "He had difficulties in the social aspect," he said. Propped against the fan, Shai hoped he could learn to idle on both legs—and to make friends with Jews as well as Arabs.

Hla Asadi هلا اسدي

It wasn't hard for Hla to learn about circus. Her cousins Hala, Ali, Manal, and Manar lived right downstairs, so she heard about it all the time.

Hla's and Hala's grandparents had built the first two floors of their limestone home on a flat stone foundation in 1967. Following local tradition, they'd added more stories, in 1995 and 2000, as their three sons married and had children.

Hla, her three brothers, and their parents lived on the fourth floor, with easy access to a rooftop patio. Sometimes, the entire extended family showed up there at mealtime.

On the floor just below them lived her uncle, his wife, and their three children. Below that were her grandparents and another uncle, who was not married. Hala's family lived on the first floor.

One day, when Hla was at home watching television, she happened to catch a show about a professional circus—a real one,

Hala and Hla's 500-Year-Old Family

According to a village sage, the Asadis have lived in Deir al-Asad since Suleiman the Magnificent conquered the area in the sixteenth century and expelled the Christians. Reminders of the Christians linger: "Deir" means "monastery," and ruins of one remain nearby. Suleiman sent a sheik, named Mohamed Asad, to secure the region. Asadis, who make up 60 percent of the village, are said to be his descendants.

not just an after-school program. "Hey, Dad!" she called. "Look at that. It's amazing."

Her father Aziz asked her if she wanted to join her cousins at their circus program.

"Of course!" she answered. But when she found out that Jewish kids also went to circus, she was confused. "At first," she said, "I didn't understand the idea." So she talked about it with her friends.

She discovered that "nobody understood about Jews" any more than she did. Her parents had a few Jewish friends, but just about everyone else she knew thought it was impossible for Jews and Arabs to get along, let alone touch each other, as they would have to do in circus classes.

Her grandmother disapproved of circus, not necessarily because of mixing with Jews but because of socializing with males. "You shouldn't be free with boys," she admonished Hla.

Of course, Hla would not be free with boys! She was a religious girl.

The Qur'an, the holy book of Islam, directs men and women to be modest and to refrain from displaying certain parts of their bodies. It also tells women to draw cloths over their heads and chests and to draw their outer garments closely around them.

People interpret this guideline in different ways. When she was eight years old, Hla told her father that she wanted to wear the hijab, the traditional headscarf worn by many Arab women. "No problem," Aziz responded. Now she wears one all the time, except when she bathes or when she's at home and her brothers aren't around. Aya Aa'mar, her closest friend, wears a *jilbab*, a coat that covers her body and disguises her shape. Only three other members of Hla's large extended family—both of her grandmothers and her cousin Manar—wear the hijab. No one in her family wears the full *jilbab*.

Despite her grandmother's objections and her own confusion about how Arabs and Jews could get along, Hla decided to give circus a try.

The coaches didn't teach skills at the first couple of classes. Instead, they talked about the need for the members of the circus to get along together, like members of a family. "The first meetings were conversation with the Jews," Hla said, "in order to strengthen coexistence, strengthen the feeling of togetherness."

They emphasized that circus, even more than other activities like soccer or orchestra, depends on unity and trust. After all, if someone is flying toward you and expects you to catch her, you'd better do it!

Hla started basic circus training, particularly elementary acrobatics, hand stands, and the splits. On her own, she worked on flexibility, her favorite activity. Hla tried to twist and bend and stretch her body like the contortionists she'd seen on television. "The first thing I tried was to do a back bend. But I'd fall on my head.... It wasn't working," she realized, "because I wasn't flexible... Nobody at circus was doing it... I wanted to do crazy shapes with my body."

Marc Rosenstein and the Galilee Circus

On Sunday evening, October 1, 2000, Marc Rosenstein stood on the front porch of his home in Shorashim, as he often did after dinner. A rabbi from Highland Park, Illinois, Marc had moved to this tiny community ten years earlier. As executive director of the Galilee Foundation for Value Education, he hoped to promote Jewish-Arab cooperation.

Marc looked across the Hilazon Valley toward a nearby Arab village. Sha'ab was close enough that he could walk there in about twenty minutes. This was not a safe night, however, for a neighborly stroll.

Sounds echo and reverberate across the stony valleys of the Galilee. On most nights, from early summer until the first rain in the fall, Marc could hear bands broadcasting outdoor wedding celebrations through loudspeakers in the Arab villages. That night, though, the loud noises he heard were rhythmic chanting in Arabic, as insistent and militant as drumbeats. He couldn't translate all of the words, but as he watched brush and forest fires blaze along the ridge above Sha'ab and other nearby Arab villages, he understood the sentiment. Possibly, Sha'ab's furious citizens were shouting "Give us back our land!" or even "Death to the Jews!"

Would they march into Shorashim, Marc wondered? *Set fire to his home? Attack him, his wife, their three children?* He had known his Arab neighbors to be peaceable, honorable, democratic citizens of Israel. Had he been deluding himself? What was happening? Whatever it was, how could he stop it?

These events occurred at the beginning of what came to be known as the Second Intifada ("uprising"). Local Arabs were expressing their frustration at being treated like second-class citizens. The Israeli government gave Jewish schools and hospitals more money than it gave the Arab institutions. Many local Jews refused to hire Arabs. Jews didn't shop in Arab stores.

Within days of the outbreak of the rioting, thirteen Galilean Arabs lay dead. The victims' families blamed Israeli police for their deaths.

In the wake of the demonstrations that had flared up in Sha'ab, Marc felt perplexed and demoralized—but also compelled to act. He wanted, somehow, to bring his Jewish friends back together with the people he had thought of as his Arab friends.

During that uneasy winter, Marc visited an American colleague in New York City, who happened to share an office with Alan Slifka. Slifka ran the Abraham Fund, a charitable foundation, and had helped found Big Apple Circus.

Marc Rosenstein

Months later, back in Israel, Marc attended a gathering of Jews who felt the same way he did about Jewish-Arab relations. They sat in a circle, brainstorming ways for Arabs and Jews to get to know each other. Maybe an arts program for kids—painting classes, an orchestra?

"Hey," Marc said, thinking of Slifka. "How about a circus? I think I know where I can get some funding."

Vision of the Galilee Foundation for Value Education

Part of the Foundation's Educational Vision states, "We believe that there cannot be harmony without knowledge of the 'other,' not only knowledge on the factual level of history and culture, but also on the human level of familiarity with his/her hopes and fears, aspirations and disappointments. This implies the need both for study and for direct personal encounter."

The group was intrigued by the idea, but no one knew anything about circuses.

Finally, after two years of pursuing various program ideas, Marc went back to his circus suggestion and obtained money from the Abraham Fund. He talked Arik Gotler-Ophir, a drama teacher who also knew nothing about circuses, into starting one. Arik hired Gilad Finkel. Then Ahmad joined the team. The Galilee Circus was born.

From the start, when nine Jewish and sixteen Arab kids signed up, the mission of the Galilee Circus was to bring together young people who would otherwise never meet or get to know each other. Although Marc didn't know the term yet, this was the definition of "social circus."

The staff wanted to balance the numbers of Jews and Arabs, but they had a hard time attracting enough Jews. Jewish schools already provided many after-school programs. But Arab schools did not. The Arab kids wanted an activity—almost any activity—and they were more willing to socialize with Jews. "The Arabs are less afraid of the Jews than the Jews are of the Arabs," Marc said.

At the end of its first season, the Galilee Circus held a few debut performances in schools and community centers in Karmiel and Deir al-Asad. A couple of hundred family members and friends of the performers came to their shows. While a few Arabs attended the shows in Karmiel, hardly any Jews "crossed the line," Marc said, to go to the performances in the Arab village.

"After holding our breaths out of concern that we really would find enough kids, that they really would be able to work together, that they really would stick out the year, that they really would give a creditable performance after only six months of practice, we all breathed easily in June." They even choked up, he admitted, "when in the curtain call, the kids stopped the music and said to the crowd, 'The Galilee Circus family thanks you with all our heart!'"

No one believed that a once-a-week circus class could do a better job of bringing peace to the Middle East than politicians and negotiators could. Nor was the class much like a real circus. But juggling and acrobatics were a start. Where would they go from here?

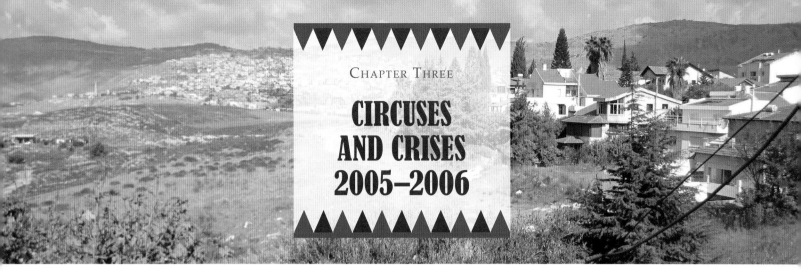

CHAPTER THREE

CIRCUSES AND CRISES 2005–2006

"Look before you leap... but leap anyway."

—Jessica's bracelet

During the summer of 2006, just before Shai was to start the Galilee Circus, he went to sleepaway camp. It was scheduled to last five days. But he ended up staying away from home for over a month.

Other kids' plans also turned topsy-turvy that summer. Roey and his family didn't intend to travel, but they left home in July and didn't return for about five weeks. Hala assumed she'd remain in Deir al-Asad, as she did every summer. But she left town as well. Hla soon wished she could escape too.

On July 12, a week after Hala turned eight, several Israeli soldiers on border patrol were killed by Hezbollah, an Arab military, political, and social organization in Lebanon. Two other soldiers were kidnapped. The Israel Defense Forces (IDF) responded by firing at targets in Lebanon. In return, Hezbollah launched rockets into northern Israel.

Initially, neither Jewish nor Arab residents paid much attention to the rockets. Skirmishes between IDF soldiers and militants in southern Lebanon occurred frequently enough to be perceived as a persistent nuisance, rather than a threat of war. The border was less than twelve miles north of Karmiel, and residents had become accustomed to the sound of rockets.

The view from the Shafrans' backyard in Karmiel

"Boom. Boom. Boom."

When the first rockets dropped, Roey was standing in line at a pharmacy in Karmiel with his mother, his sister, and his brother. "You heard three explosions," Roey said. "Boom. Boom. Boom. Really soft."

People around him were matter-of-fact. He heard someone say that they were just rockets from Lebanon.

"No one thought it would be big," Roey said. "In the Jewish villages that surround this mountain, it was routine that missiles fall. People didn't really notice."

But on the drive home, Roey saw a father and daughter running down the street. He rolled down the car window and heard an air-raid siren. That meant the Shafrans had fifteen seconds to shield themselves from the incoming rocket.

Orly stopped the car in the middle of the road, and the family leaped out and scrambled to the nearest public bomb shelter. Once inside, they felt secure. They spent the next couple of hours chatting with neighbors, then drove back home.

The siren sounded again the next day. Roey and his family piled into the shelter in their basement, which his mother had been using as a pottery studio. Still, the Shafrans continued to believe, as Roey said, "It's nothing. It's probably going to stop tomorrow. It's not going to be a war."

The family felt relatively safe because the rockets that they kept hearing were not landing in Karmiel or in any of the surrounding Jewish villages. Either Hezbollah's aim was off or its munitions experts weren't yet using enough propulsion to reach their intended targets. Instead, Roey's father recalled, the rockets, heavily loaded with steel ball bearings, were hitting the Arab towns of Biane, Deir al-Asad, and Majd al-Krum, where they killed people and destroyed buildings.

"It Was a Very, Very Tense Time"

When they heard the air-raid sirens, many people in Deir al-Asad scurried up to their flat rooftops to see what was happening. Salam

WATCH OUT FOR FLYING KIDS!

Hezbollah

Hezbollah, which means "Party of God," is a political and religious organization formed in the early 1980s by Shi'ite Muslims.

In 1982, Israel sent forces into southern Lebanon to stop terrorist attacks by the Palestine Liberation Organization. Hezbollah was formed with the intent of ending the resulting Israeli military occupation. Through a variety of strategies, including suicide bombings, hijackings, and kidnappings of Jewish soldiers and civilians, Hezbollah succeeded. The IDF withdrew its soldiers in 2000.

The United States considers Hezbollah a terrorist organization and holds it responsible for attacking its embassy in Beirut in 1983.

Abu Zeid, Hala's aunt, believed the scuffles would end soon, just as Roey's family assumed. "When the war started," she said, "we didn't think it would be as difficult as it was." Soon she changed her mind, just as the Shafrans did. "Once the rockets fell on our village, we got scared," she said.

Public air-raid shelters like those in Jewish towns are not available in Arab villages, but many homes have what is called a "safe room." Unlike public air-raid shelters, though, safe rooms are not reinforced. They are windowless spaces, preferably interior ones, on the south side of a building since the rockets come from the north. If one of Hezbollah's rockets fell onto or even close to a house, it could severely damage it. The house might even tumble down the cliff on which it sits. Hala and Hla's house has a safe room on the first floor, but it had not been well maintained.

Salam owned a home in Beersheva, a town 140 miles to the south—too far for the rockets to reach. When bombardment started that summer, Salam left for Beersheva and took Hala with her. They remained there for ten days.

The rest of the family stayed in Deir al-Asad. "I spent a lot of time in the safe room," Hla said. "It was a very, very tense time. It lasted for a whole month. It felt like forever." Her parents didn't want the children to be frightened, so they provided games to try to distract them. Hla passed the time playing cards with her brothers.

Although they were terrified by the rockets, the girls and their families felt ambivalent about Hezbollah's actions. As Arabs, they sympathized with the Arabs in Lebanon, including members of Hezbollah. Yet, as Israelis, they didn't want Hezbollah to attack their country.

"All of us have complex feelings about all of this," Salam explained. "It's not really easy for us to say that we hate Hezbollah. But it's also not easy for us to say that it's good for them to shoot rockets here…. We don't want to be hit with rockets, but we don't want them [Lebanese] to be shot at [by Jews]."

Other people in her village were proud that their Arab "brothers" in Lebanon were taking action against the Jewish people. Jews had confiscated their property—their country, they believed—in 1948. They felt it was time to retaliate, to eject the Jews, and to reclaim the land.

Hala did not support the attacks. She would be starting circus soon, and she'd have to face Jews—Jews whom other Arabs were trying to kill.

"I Don't Want to Stay Here!"

Israeli media did not announce the exact locations where Hezbollah's rockets landed. They didn't want the organization to know that they were falling short of their targets. Nevertheless, within two days of the start of the attacks, Hezbollah's aim improved.

While the Shafrans were eating lunch at home on July 15, Roey's father heard a whistling sound. "Run to the shelter!" he shouted. "Run to the shelter!"

Seconds later, a bomb thudded into Roey's backyard. By the time he and his family reached the stairs to their shelter, a second bomb hit nearby.

"We heard all the windows in the house shattering," Roey said. "We felt the shock wave."

The family locked the massive steel door to the shelter. Fortunately, they had already removed his mother's worktables and pottery wheel and laid out mattresses on the floor, just in case.

Roey jumped onto a mattress and covered his head with his arms. But he could still hear his sister crying and, at the same time, laughing hysterically. "We're going now!" he demanded. "I don't want to stay here." His parents agreed that they needed to escape Karmiel as soon as it seemed safe to do so.

Just then, a policeman banged on their door, yelling, "Get out! Get out! Your house is on fire!"

The Shafrans ran back upstairs, where they discovered that the fire was a small one and only in the backyard. But shrapnel

The entrance to the Shafrans' bomb shelter

41

The Second Lebanon War

The Second Lebanon War, as it came to be known, lasted for a total of thirty-four days. In response to Hezbollah's actions, the IDF deployed its army, navy, and air force. Hezbollah, in turn, escalated rocket attacks. Almost 200 struck in or near Karmiel and surrounding Jewish towns, destroying nearly a dozen homes. Several residents of Karmiel were injured, but no one was killed. In Deir al-Asad, no homes were damaged but many people were injured, and two were killed by a bomb: Maryam Assadi, an acquaintance of Hala's Aunt Salam, and Maryam's son.

Following negotiations with the United Nations, the Israeli government and Hezbollah agreed to a cease-fire, which took effect on August 14, 2006.

and shards of glass littered the floors; a steel ball bearing had been driven into a window frame.

Within half an hour, the Shafrans had packed up their belongings, including the two family dogs, and headed to Haifa, twenty-seven miles to the east and, more importantly, thirty miles from the Lebanese border. "Haifa is far from Lebanon," Roey said. They spent that night in the basement of Roey's aunt and uncle's home, where they felt more secure.

But the next morning, they heard another explosion. This time, it was Roey who became hysterical. "No one believed it would come to Haifa," he said. They fled again, to another relative's home, this time in Tel Aviv, fifty-seven miles to the south. Sixteen family members squeezed together for six weeks.

Despite the dangers, Roey's father returned to Karmiel. He had to go to work. Some of his colleagues were Arabs, and, despite the war, they continued to work alongside each other. On weekends, he drove to Tel Aviv to see his family.

"I Froze and Screamed"

Shai and his fellow campers were evacuated to Tel Aviv, and then after a week to Modi'in, where he stayed with family friends. Meanwhile, his parents and sister were still in Atzmon. He worried about them at first, but then felt reassured, knowing that they'd be safe in their home shelter.

The children finally returned home the second week in August. Shai's sister showed him where a piece of a rocket had fallen outside the gates to Atzmon. Otherwise, the villagers and their property were unharmed. Until the cease-fire, Shai and his sister alternated between their rooms and the shelter, keeping board games going in both places.

Hala was ecstatic to see her family again. Hla finally had someone else to play with besides her brothers.

Roey remained so traumatized by the war that he soon developed phobias—irrational fears. His mother suggested that

the family visit a nature preserve. What caught Roey's attention at the preserve were hundreds, possibly thousands, of dragonflies, hovering and darting over the lake. "I froze and screamed," he said. "My father caught me and hugged me really hard but I couldn't move." Roey's fear of bugs practically paralyzed him. "It was really bad. It really stopped me from living my life."

They returned to Karmiel, and he managed to go back to school when it started two-and-a-half weeks later. So did Hala and Hla in Deir al-Asad and Shai in Misgav.

Several weeks after that, the Galilee Circus reopened. Despite his traumas, Roey returned to circus, as did Hala's sisters and brother, along with other Arab and Jewish kids. Shai and Hala attended for the first time.

No one at circus talked about the war. Or about what they had done that summer. Or about where they had hidden. Or about their fears, especially not their fears of each other.

"Once we get to circus," Hala explained, "there's an agreement. We don't talk about such issues. Discussions don't enter into the circus."

"The Lowest-Ceilinged Circus School in the World"

In August 2005, Tim Holst, the talent scout for Ringling Brothers Barnum & Bailey Circus, watched the Arches perform at the annual American Youth Circus Organization Festival in San Francisco. He was so impressed that he invited the troupe to perform before the main show when Ringling came to St. Louis in November.

The hometown crowd, Jessica said, "went wild!" After the show, the young performers got a private backstage tour. In a newsletter to Circus Harmony's supporters and parents, Jessica speculated that maybe some day "one of our young stars may become a feature act with Ringling Brothers!"

Throughout the fall, winter, and spring, the Arches performed for the general public four times a week in the circus's small facility on the third floor of City Museum. The ceiling there was so low that it was a big disadvantage for flyers.

43

*Jessica spots Shaina in
Circus Harmony's original ring*

Hoping for a space with higher ceilings, Jessica wrote in a newsletter, "Our aerialists can't wait to stop scraping the floor, and our acrobats are tired of hitting the ceiling." If a better space ever opened up, she said, "we may have to stop billing ourselves as the lowest-ceilinged circus school in the world!"

Still, the Arches had a blast, impressing audiences not only at the museum but also at off-site performances for schools, festivals, churches, and benefits. As a group, they were thriving, but some of its members were struggling.

"He Died Right by My Bed"

Late one night, Iking's Uncle Miles got locked out of the house he shared with Iking, his seven other nieces and nephews, and their grandmother. Miles went up the street to stay at a cousin's house. While he slept, the cousin stole Miles's money. After arguing about the theft for a week, Miles retaliated by taking his cousin's shoes home with him.

"My cousin came down the street with a gun," Iking said, "shot [Miles] in our living room [which] was right next to my bedroom.... So, he died right in our house, in the living room, right by my bed."

Iking couldn't face living in the place where his favorite uncle had been murdered. He moved to Jessica's house for about a month, placing his toothbrush in the holder above his name on her bathroom wall.

Not long after Miles's death, Iking's grandmother moved the family from the Walnut Park East section of St. Louis to Penrose. The areas were only two miles apart, but Walnut Park East was Crips territory—Iking's gang. Penrose was the territory of the Bloods, a rival gang, two of whose members were also Arches— Terrance ("T-Roc") Robinson and Melvin Diggs.

"It was really dangerous to get on the bus," Iking said. "I never went outside because I probably would have…messy stuff would have happened."

One day, Iking was hanging out at City Museum with a group of teenagers. A guy brushed against him. Iking didn't know him, and wasn't sure if it was a gang move. Hypersensitive to the possibility of violence, Iking swung his fist. When the security guard tried to break up the fight, Iking ran off. But the guard recognized him and called the police. Iking was relieved when the police merely drove him home, without even giving him a lecture.

Helicopter

Helicopter (pictured on page 47) is an especially challenging trick. The bases must work in unison to throw and rotate the flyer into a circle, like the blade of a helicopter propeller. Meanwhile, the flyer has to remain completely tight, but that is almost impossible because centrifugal force can splay his arms and legs. "When your body is spinning so fast," Alex says, "the flyer's limbs will hit the bases and hurt—a lot."

"You Want to Be Able to Keep Doing the Trick"

Practicing and taking classes at least four times a week, the Arches threw, caught, flew, bounced, contorted, spun, and hefted themselves and each other until Wishbone, Airplane, Helicopter, Pyramid, and many other routines became signature acts.

Generally, the larger, stronger kids served as bases—they stayed on the ground—and the shorter, lighter ones acted as flyers—they climbed onto shoulders and were pitched into the air. But just in case, everyone had to master everything. "We all learned all the parts that we could," Alex explained. "You have to learn various parts because otherwise, if someone falls or if someone is hurt, you want to be able to replace them. You want to be able to keep doing the trick."

"I Was Disappointed That I Couldn't Do More"

Shaina had spent the past year getting used to yet another new school, this one almost 300 miles away from the place she considered home. She played violin in her school orchestra and went out for track. Yet, shy, private, and unsure how long her mother would stay in Rock Island, she was reluctant to make new friends. By spring, she yearned to return to St. Louis, knowing that the Arches would be getting ready for Circus Flora.

At the beginning of the summer, her father drove to Illinois and brought her back to St. Louis. Since Shaina hadn't practiced with the Arches all year, she couldn't perform. But Jessica let her "tumble out"—that is, handspring out of the ring with the Arches during the finale of each show—as if she were still a member of the troupe. "I was a little disappointed that I couldn't do more," Shaina admitted.

"Most Stupefying"

In February 2006, Kellin entered the 28th Annual Groundhog Day Juggling Festival and Competition in Atlanta. He had worked with Richard for two months on his act. For a while, people called

The Arches perform Helicopter

him "Incorrigible Kellin" because he did—or didn't do—whatever he pleased.

Just before Kellin went on, Richard had a final talk with him. "You can do the act that we've been working on," Richard told him. "Or, you can do whatever you want. It's up to you."

Kellin paused and pondered, then said, "I've decided to do the act we've been working on." He and Richard shook hands.

Kellin unicycled into the performance area carrying a fake pizza on an outsized spatula. Then he juggled kitchen equipment, including pots, a fork, a ladle, fake apples, wire whisks, potatoes, and eggs. For his finish trick, he juggled knives while he balanced on a giant orange globe. Once again, Kellin beat out professional jugglers, winning the "Most Stupefying" prize and a coveted statuette of Punxatawny Phil.

"You Learn to Fall"

Though they were young, the Arches weren't amateurs. Starring in as many as 400 shows a year, they were featured as guest performers with America's top circuses when they came to town and paid for their appearances. The Arches had continued to work with Circus Flora even after the professional troupe withdrew its support for the youth program.

David said, "The Arches are a really important part of the show. They've grown not to be just a school act.... They're very professionally important to us." Now, David suggested they try something new: an equestrian act.

Jessica picked out five Arches who were not only daring but also were willing to muck out stalls. Only one of them, Claire Kuciejczyk-Kernan, had ever encountered a horse up close. Ranging in age from thirteen to sixteen, the equestrians were the only youth circus troupe, as far as they knew, trained in bareback riding.

Before the riders could learn the tricks, called voltige, they had to learn how to fall off safely. "You learn to fall *in* the ring and not *out*," Elliana said, speaking from experience, "because 'out' means 'people,' and 'in' means 'sawdust.' It's not a fun fall [to land on the audience]."

In May and June 2006, the Arches presented three full-length, professional-strength acts: the equestrian program; a duet on the lyra; and a fifteen-person tumbling, acrobatics, and juggling routine. First, they performed at the Spoleto Festival, a prestigious international arts festival in South Carolina. The next month the Arches returned to St. Louis to put on ten shows a week with Circus Flora, for three weeks straight.

Kellin performs at the Groundhog Day Juggling Festival and Competition

In July—the same month that Hala, Hla, Roey, and Shai were dodging rockets—the Arches were special guests at UniverSOUL Circus. This is the only circus in the country that is owned and operated by African-Americans.

Within one month during the fall of 2006, they not only performed for Ringling and for Cirque du Soleil, but they also staged their annual show.

That year's production, named for a musical term like all the others, was called *Glissando*. The Italian word refers to gliding between two notes. At Circus Harmony, Jessica said, it referred to "how our youth circus performers glide between being ordinary children and extraordinary circus performers."

"It's Too Dangerous!"

One day, Marc Googled "youth circus" out of curiosity. He was stunned when he scrolled down his computer screen and saw hundreds of links from all over the world. He had assumed that he had invented the notion of kids doing circus tricks.

Marc clicked on a number of the links, including one for Circus Harmony, where he read a startling headline:

Circus Salaam Shalom
20 young Muslim and Jewish kids put on a really good circus show with everything from juggling to trapeze.

There was even a photograph of Muslim girls in headscarves balancing on other kids' backs, just like in his circus program. The article explained that Jessica Hentoff had organized the one-time show as part of her community outreach program.

Marc e-mailed half a dozen youth circuses, "probably out of the ulterior motive," he admitted, "that they could help us raise money." A few responded with halfhearted answers.

Jessica, however, wrote back at length. She was Jewish and wanted to promote cross-cultural connections. She'd even spent the summer in Israel when she was sixteen years old.

Elliana, age 17, performs voltige at Circus Flora, June 2009

49

"We started this e-mail romance," Marc said.

In the fall of 2006, Marc wrote to her: "Wouldn't it be neat if you could send kids here for a week or so? It would be great PR. It would be great for my circus."

"NO!" Jessica answered. "It's too dangerous." Even if the kids hadn't been watching the news about the Middle East that summer, she had. Jessica was delighted to have children walk a tightwire, hang by their heels from a trapeze, and vault on and off of cantering horses, but not tumble into a war zone.

"I don't want to try and convince people because I don't believe in that," Marc told Jessica. "If you want to come, you'll come. We had 10,000 kids here last summer, and they all went home fine. But, you'll do what you're going to do."

About 2,000 of the kids that Marc referred to were teenagers, most of them American, who participated in another program offered by the Galilee Foundation for Value Education. This program conducts study tours for visiting youth as well as opportunities for young Jews from abroad to talk with young Arabs in the Galilee. No one, Marc pointed out, had been injured.

"You'll Never Juggle Knives"

While she was struggling with her decision about the trip to Israel, Jessica got a visit from an old acquaintance. When she was an eighteen-year-old debutante, Elizabeth "Bunny" Herring had run off to Ringling and worked as a showgirl for three years.

Now, sixty-two years later, Bunny wanted to return to that daring lifestyle. "I promised my parents when I joined the circus that I wouldn't do anything aerial," she told Jessica. "But they're gone now. Do you think I could do it now? Or is it too late?"

Jessica noticed that her newest and oldest student had a tattoo on her ankle. It read, *Esse Quam Videre*—Latin for "To be rather than to seem to be." The phrase reminded Jessica of her bracelet engraved with the words, "Look before you leap...but leap anyway."

That fall, Jessica was the featured speaker at the first-ever Social Circus Conference in America. As she prepared her talk, she thought about her circus's—her life's—stated mission: "We help children defy gravity, soar with confidence, and leap over social barriers, all at the same time."

"If you spend your whole life thinking, 'What if, what if?' you'll never juggle knives," Jessica realized. "You'll never do a somersault. You'll never get out of bed. You can talk yourself into not leaving your cocoon. You have to look at 'Why not?'… If I'm saying, 'We're a social circus and [we're] building a bridge between cultures,' how can I say 'no' to something which is so much the very image of a cultural divide, [the] Arab-Jewish?"

Maybe the Arches could go to Israel, after all. But, before she could commit to such a costly and potentially dangerous undertaking, she needed to talk with Marc. "Before I was going across the ocean," said, "I wanted to meet this person, to see him face-to-face."

"I don't think we're ambassadors. I think we're kids with a passion for something."

—Elliana Hentoff-Killian

I n the winter of 2007, Jessica flew to New York to visit her father. Marc also happened to be in town. The two circus directors arranged to meet for lunch at Grand Central Station near a kiosk that sold kosher food he could eat.

Jessica brought Elliana, Keaton, and Kellin. Marc found the kids fussy and uncooperative. Keaton, who was sick, threw up.

Jessica listened to Marc's description of the Galilee Circus and its mission. Face-to-face, she could see that he was a responsible person. She agreed to take the Arches to Israel after all. "This is either going to be an amazing adventure," Jessica decided, "or a heck of a news story. Here these kids go over for world peace—and they get killed! I just gave it over to the universe."

"Israel Better Be in St. Louis!"

But how many of the Arches' parents would agree to give their children over to the universe—or, at least, to her? Would her willingness to take her own children to Israel be enough to convince other anxious parents?

She decided to tell the kids first. "I know that's not the best thing to do," she later confessed.

Jessica wasn't sure how many of her performers—with the possible exception of Michel Simmons, a faithful Bible reader—could even find Israel on a map. Iking hoped the Israelis would all

Backstage at Circus Harmony

speak English. "If not, I won't be saying much," he said. Lemond Carmickle's first question was, "Can we ride camels?"

Of course, all of the Arches wanted to go. They ran home, excited to tell their parents about the "amazing experience" they could have.

When Shaina's half brother Lil Donald asked his mother if he could go to Israel for two weeks, she blurted out, "Israel? Israel better be in St. Louis!" Lil Donald did not get permission to go. But Shaina did—their father, Big Donald, and Shaina's mother both thought the trip would be a good opportunity for her.

Alex's parents had already planned a family vacation that summer. She argued with them, but they refused to change their plans.

Michel's parents didn't want him to go either, but his father talked with some friends who convinced him to change his mind. After further conversations, all of the other parents also agreed.

Eleven Arches, Jessica, Diane, a juggling coach, one father, and a documentary film crew started to get ready. All they needed was $45,000. And every one of the Arches going on the trip had to get a passport.

Jessica and Marc created fund-raising appeals, using the slogans "Harmony Through Handsprings" and "Peace Through Pyramids." They made their goal known in newsletters and messages to supporters and in proposals to foundations.

This cross-cultural, country-connecting circus will demonstrate in a breathtaking way what can happen when people of different nationalities and backgrounds build something together. These are only children—but they have a lot to teach the rest of the world.

Suggested amounts for donations ranged from $100 to cover the cost of a passport, to $3000, the amount needed to sponsor one performer for the whole trip. To display how much they had raised—and how much more they needed to raise—Jessica crafted a giant poster that showed their progress using colorful images of tumbling acrobats.

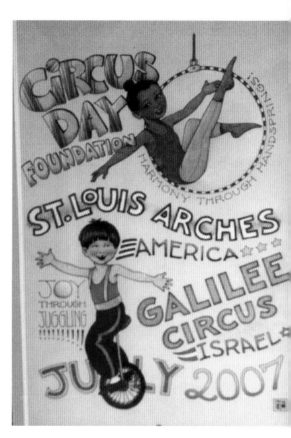

A fund-raising poster created by St. Louis artist Mary Englebreit

53

The Arches also raised money themselves, putting on benefit shows. "We were totally scraping in St. Louis," Jessica said, "trying to raise that money."

"We're Knocking Down Your Office"

In the midst of the harried fund-raising campaign, Jessica had to pack up and move the circus. Bob had decided to build a new kitchen in the City Museum—directly in front of the circus's space. One of the kitchen's walls, thrown up almost overnight, now blocked the entrance to that area.

Jessica wasn't prepared to relocate immediately. She wanted to work out a few details with Bob first, though she didn't always get her way. Easy access and special seats for handicapped audience members? Never happened. Blue carpeting? He'd only pay for red. Although the new space would have a higher ceiling, the entrance to the ring was too narrow to accommodate the circus's giant rolling globe. And Bob had no idea if the windows that surrounded nearly half of the ring were composed of shatterproof safety glass—an absolute necessity.

Yet in spite of the obstacles, less than a month later—after Bob jacked up the ceiling an additional four feet and widened the entryway for the globe—Circus Harmony performed its first show in its new location.

Jessica's office remained in its old area on the other side of the building. Then one day, she got a call. "You have two hours," a construction worker warned, "and then we're knocking down your office."

Jessica moved.

"I Had No Limits"

The Arches kept practicing, improving, and performing throughout the spring of 2007. Iking was tackling a Double Back—two midair back tucks—from solid ground, rather than relying on a mini-tramp to help him with momentum and elevation. In thirty-seven years in the ring, Warren, who was now coaching at Circus

Harmony, had only seen one acrobat accomplish this trick. When Iking finally perfected the Double Back, just before the troupe left for Israel, he said, "I felt like I had no limits…. Any trick was reachable."

At the end of April Jessica wrote Gilad, laying out the Arches' many skills.

All our children can at least juggle three objects. We use balls, rings, clubs, and knives…. Some of the boys can juggle five balls and rings and a couple can juggle four and five clubs. Most pass six and some can pass seven. Some of the boys are very good at diabolo and can do double diabolo and toss and catch with a forward roll or back handspring. They all pass diabolos. We have three boys who do rolla and can do the two-high stack…. One of the boys coming does a nice hand-balancing act on chairs. Most of the girls specialize in aerial. One also is working on hula hooping…. Some of the boys also do trapeze. The girls do lyra, web, and some silks. All the children do tumbling (everyone can do back handspring, most do somersaults, some do twists) and partner acrobatics. All do rolling globe…. Several can unicycle and some have done a bicycle act. Some can walk tightwire although we do not yet have an act of this and one is working on slack wire. We do a lot with mini-trampoline. I would say some are advanced. Most are intermediate level.

Warren Bacon spots Iking as he performs a Double Back

By comparison, the Galilee kids' skills seemed paltry. Gilad sent Jessica a list:

We work a lot with different juggling skills, some acrobatics, tightrope, little bit of clowning, and hope to start next year with trapeze and tissue. ["Tissue" is what the Israelis called the aerial act "silks."]

Shai was working on juggling balls as well as unicycling and staff twirling. Manar and Manal could juggle three balls and

WATCH OUT FOR FLYING KIDS!

balance on each other's knees. Roey could roll, toss, and catch a diabolo. A few of the kids had tried out the tightwire. Clearly, they were far behind the Arches.

"Out of the Conflict and into the World of Circus"

By early May, the Arches had received contributions from a range of donors, including members of Circus Harmony's board of directors, a local synagogue, a regional arts commission, and even Cirque du Soleil. But two weeks before their departure, they had raised only $30,000. Despite her earlier goal of $45,000, Jessica announced that this would be enough to pay for the trip.

But it would be tight. There would be other expenses on top of the travel. The Arches wanted to purchase gifts for their Israeli hosts. Since they knew the Galilee Circus was hoping to start doing aerials, they decided to donate a trapeze. And for good measure, they would also give them a globe, a Spanish web, juggling props, books, and a poster.

Costumes were a concern too. "Do we need to worry about the girls showing their legs?" Jessica asked. Marc responded that leotards were fine for shows but the girls should be prepared to cover their heads, shoulders, and legs when visiting mosques, synagogues, and other holy sites.

In Israel, the Galilee Circus Parents Committee organized homestays for the visitors. Hala's parents signed up. So did Roey's. The Parents Committee found chaperones and guides for sightseeing tours. Shai's parents agreed to serve in both roles, and his mother arranged to travel around Israel with the circuses for a week.

In St. Louis, a circus mother packed small toiletry kits with shampoo and toothpaste for everyone. A local rabbi talked to the travelers about Israeli hip-hop, ghettoes, and graffiti. He and a circus father also gave a token amount of money to each one for the Jewish tradition of *tzedakah*—charity—asking them to give the money to someone in need in Israel.

The passports for Kellin, Keaton, Elliana, Jessica, and Renaldo ("Junior") Williams hadn't arrived yet. "You alternate between

being in a total panic," Jessica said, "and going, Nope. They're going to come."

The Americans were excited; hardly any of them had ever been out of the country. The Israeli kids were excited too; unlike the Arches, they had never seen a live circus show or met a circus performer.

The St. Louis Arches and their entourage at the airport before departing for Israel. Front row: Rianna Glazier-Snow, Jessica, Anthony Stiles. Back row: Shaina, Michel Simmons, Keaton, Junior, Alex, Diane, Elliana, Matt, Claire Kuciejczyk-Kernan, Lemond, Deon White, Iking, Dan Glazier.

"We didn't know what to expect," Shai said. Gilad warned them that the Americans were sensitive about race and that no one should "use any words that may offend them."

The Americans also remained anxious about their safety. Some of the boys joked about stepping on land mines. Knowing that Israel "is surrounded with a bunch of enemies," Kellin expected to see many people carrying weapons.

Jessica assured them that "everyone who's been to Israel swears that, once you're in Israel, it doesn't feel like there's a war." Nevertheless, she ordered her mother-in-law not to watch the news while they were in the Middle East.

Summarizing the purpose of their trip for the media, Jessica stated, "We're going as peace ambassadors." Marc added, "We hope that the St. Louis Arches' visit here will help draw us completely out of the conflict and into the world of circus.… Our own goal for our kids in the Galilee is to raise the circus out of being a Jewish-Arab circus to just being a circus."

Some of the Arches had a different perspective. "I don't think we're ambassadors," Elliana said just before they left—shortly after her passport finally arrived. "I think we're kids with a passion for something. And we're going to be sharing that passion with other kids."

On July 8, Alex and Lil Donald showed up at the airport at 7:30 in the morning to wish the rest of the troupe bon voyage. Alex was bored waiting for everyone to check their luggage, so she performed her partner act with Junior. Their routine attracted attention from other travelers. Pretty soon, passersby were asking the Arches where they were heading. Even people who were not venturing to Israel learned that these black and white, urban and suburban performers were about to add Israeli Arabs and Jews to their mix.

"They Looked Funny"

After a two-and-a-half-hour flight from St. Louis to New Jersey, a layover, another twelve-hour flight to Tel Aviv, and a two-hour bus ride across Israel, the Arches and their entourage pulled into a parking lot in Karmiel. The searing sun, high overhead, told them it was around noon, but their jet-lagged bodies reminded them that it was barely four in the morning in St. Louis.

They were met by the Galilee Circus performers and their parents. Like sixth-graders at a school dance, the two groups stared at each other. The Arches hung together, sweltering in their black long-sleeved jackets and pants. The Israelis wore T-shirts and shorts—except for Manar, who wore a modest long-sleeved top, pants, and a tightly wrapped headscarf.

"We couldn't convince them that the point is to go on and not make the other person lose."

—Shai Ben Yosef

The view from Hala and Hla's roof in Deir al-Asad

"Nothing happened," Roey said. "There was no interaction."

"They looked funny to us," Ali Hasarme explained, "because some were so black." The sixteen-year-old Arab boy had never seen an African-American before. Nor had he seen many white Americans. "They were strange, new, different."

The Arches couldn't tell who was Jewish and who was Arab. All of the Israelis looked and sounded foreign to them. "It was weird seeing signs and hearing people talk in a different language," Shaina said. She didn't plan to make close friends with the Israelis, so the language barrier did not pose a problem for her. "I wasn't really concerned," she said. "I just either stayed to myself or only talked to the Arches."

Hebrew might not have seemed quite so strange to Shaina as it did to most of the Arches. She had picked up bits of it in St. Louis. "I was staying the night at Jessica's house almost every Friday night.… Saturday morning, I went with her [to synagogue]. I learned part of the alphabet and some words of Hebrew."

Jessica's children had been taught the sounds of the Hebrew alphabet. They attended synagogue to prepare for their bar and bat mitzvahs, the ceremonies that welcome Jews to adulthood at age thirteen. Their father is not Jewish, and they did not feel strongly attached to their heritage. Kellin even declared that his religion was juggling.

Arabic was utterly foreign to all of the Arches, regardless of their religious background or linguistic training. "It was hard for most of the Americans," Shai said, "that most of us didn't speak English. But, since we're Arabs and Jews, we're used to not understanding every word the other person says. We didn't really care. It seemed kind of weird that they had a problem not understanding us."

Shai reached into the bus's baggage hold, pulled out three colorful balls, and started juggling. Using a well-known juggler's trick, Lemond "stole" the balls from Shai and continued juggling with them. Then, Noam stole the balls from Lemond.

"We didn't talk yet," Roey said. "We just juggled."

Lemond and Noam Davidovich juggle

"Ewww!"

By the time everyone got onto the bus, they had made some effort to communicate. Jessica insisted that each of them sit with someone they didn't know during the forty-five minute drive to Kibbutz Sasa, their first stop.

Shai had learned some English by watching American cartoons on television. He chatted with Keaton about Greek mythology. Many of the others, however, merely shrugged and pointed. Kellin threw peanuts at his brother.

The Americans' discomfort grew when they stared at the offerings in the kibbutz's communal cafeteria. Practically the only

61

What's a Kibbutz?

A kibbutz is a residential community in Israel where the members, called kibbutzniks, share the work and the proceeds from their work. They also generally share communal services, such as dining facilities and child care. The first kibbutzim were agricultural. Today, their work might be industrial or technological.

Kibbutz Sasa, located just a mile south of Israel's border with Lebanon, was founded in 1949, on the site of an Arab village that was defeated by the IDF during the War of Independence/the *Nakba*. In addition to tending fruit orchards and dairy herds, the kibbutz builds armored cars and airplanes; makes cleaning products; and operates a hostel for visitors, who can use its well-equipped gymnasium.

recognizable items were rice and green beans. Even the bread, called pita, was odd to them—round and flat with a pocket in the middle. What looked like pale gray goop turned out to be a spread made of eggplant mashed with garlic. Even worse was the tan glop called hummus, a combination of chickpeas blended with sesame paste.

"Ewww! No, no, no, no," one of the Arches exclaimed. "Hummus was one of the worst things I tasted." Iking claimed that he was under doctor's orders to eat only Big Macs.

While several Arches, including Kellin and Elliana, experimented and found that they enjoyed the Middle Eastern cuisine, others pulled snack bars out of their backpacks. The local Jewish and Arab kids, on the other hand, ate the foods, which were familiar to all of them. Despite their different backgrounds, their diets were similar.

"I Can't Do This"

After lunch, the two troupes and their coaches hauled their equipment into the kibbutz's gymnasium for their first joint practice session. The facilities were spacious, high ceilinged, and brightly lit, with tiers of alternating red and blue seats along one long side. But the Americans were dismayed when they saw the Galilee Circus's gear.

Rather than regulation mats, they found thin, old-fashioned mattresses filled with horsehair. "It was not a comfortable mat," Shaina observed. "When you'd land, you could feel the ground through the mat." Shaina, who came from one of the least advantaged backgrounds of all of the Arches, thought, "being American, we had better things than they did.... We were more privileged than they were. I was grateful."

Jessica looked at the sagging mini-tramp and pronounced it "just horrible." She had told Gilad that the Arches use this piece of equipment as the jumping-off point for a lot of their tricks, so the Galilee Circus had borrowed one for the occasion. None of the

Israelis had ever tried it. Its webbing was so stretched out of shape, the "bed" nearly sagged to the ground.

The American coaches explained the technique, and Manar tried to follow their instructions—run, jump, bounce, land. With no momentum or height and off-balance, she sank and staggered, nearly toppling over.

"Keep your arms up," Matt Viverito, an Arch, advised Manar. That way, she wouldn't fall forward.

"I can't do this," she complained.

"We're Not Really a Circus"

Then it was Iking's turn. The mini-tramp didn't faze him, however. Knees flexed, arms up, and core engaged, he rebounded with enough height to execute a forward tuck and even recover from his slightly wobbly landing with a back handspring. The Israelis gaped.

The next two Arches did successive forward tucks. In another run, Iking soared into a split-leg side somersault. Even Shaina, who had not practiced with the Arches all year, launched into a series of tight handsprings, polished off with a forward tuck. She was pleased when the Israelis stared at her with awe, just as they had at Iking.

Roey shook his head. *I'm not good enough*, he thought. Then, he had a devastating realization. *We're not really a circus.*

The Arches also faced challenges when they tried out equipment that was new to them. Keaton sat on a tall stool while Manar and Mysa strapped his lower legs into their yard-high stilts. "This is easy," he exclaimed, strolling a few feet across the gym floor. Moments later, he thudded onto his stomach and kneepads. Arms and legs splayed and unable to stand up, he cried, "Help!" Manar and Mysa came to his rescue.

And that was just the first day.

"I Don't Want to Do It"

On the second day, Elliana demonstrated trapeze, using the one that the Arches had brought with them as a gift. Several Galilee kids watched in amazement as she went through the paces of a basic routine.

Elliana and Shirel Mondrik practice trapeze

Even after the mini-tramp fiasco, Manar gamely tried out another apparatus that was brand new to her. She stood on the mattress and grasped the trapeze bar. As soon as she lifted her feet, her body swung forward. She winced and let go, dropping to the floor. "That really hurts," she said, shaking her head and walking off the mat. "I never learned to do this. Never." She made it clear that she never intended to, either.

"Their circus skills were…super low," Iking pronounced. "We surpassed them tremendously, in so many areas. We were so much better than them—not to feel cocky." The Israelis, the Americans noticed, didn't even know how to style.

"Head up!" Jessica commanded. "Chest open. Right hand at ten o'clock. Left at two." Ta da! She told them to do that at the end of every trick, even when they bungled.

Unlike Iking, Shai noticed a balance between the two groups. The Arches' specialties, he said, "are acrobatics. And our specialties are juggling. So, we can both teach each other stuff we don't know."

Amit Gelman, one of the Galilee coaches, demonstrated how to twirl the staff. Flicking his wrists and rotating his hands and arms, he spun the staff over his head and behind his back and flipped it from hand to hand. He explained that maintaining control of the two-pound pole would be especially important when each end was filled with a flammable liquid and set aflame.

Gritting his teeth, Iking slowly and awkwardly revolved the staff a few times, then let it drop. "I don't want to learn it," he said. "If it's not diabolo or tumbling, I can't do it." Just in case he hadn't made his point clearly enough, he added, "I don't like doing it. I don't want to do it."

Shaina tried it briefly and then quit too. "I kept hitting myself in the head," she complained. After that, only a couple of Arches even dared to try poi.

"I Don't Want to Fall on My Head"

That evening—just when the members of each troupe were thoroughly frustrated by their inability to learn each other's tricks—it was time to put on a show. Jessica announced that the combined "Galilee Arches" were to perform for the families who lived at the kibbutz.

The Arches hadn't even recuperated from jet lag and the eight-hour difference in time zones. "Putting a show together in a short period of time is really hard," Iking grumbled, "'cause you gotta communicate with each other, and we don't speak the same language."

During rehearsals, Jessica paired up her professional-caliber Arches with the rookies from the Galilee. She directed Elliana to put together a dual trapeze act with eleven-year-old Shirel Mondrik and an acrobatics routine with Ali.

Elliana fretted that performing with newbies would be dangerous. "I don't want to fall on my head," she lamented.

Jessica dismissed her concerns. "And I *so* wanted you to fall on your head!"

Elliana hung by her knees from the trapeze next to Shirel while Jessica tugged, stretched, and molded the Israeli girl into a variety of positions.

To prep for a joint acrobatics act, Lemond asked another Israeli how much she weighed. Not understanding him, she laughed. "Answer!" he demanded. She laughed again and walked away. Frustrated, Lemond shook his head.

Because the Galilee kids had never done "work on shoulders," Jessica needed to teach them how to climb onto each other. If the two circuses were going to perform together, the Galilee kids would have to learn to do a Two-High—a flyer standing atop a base.

Planning a Show

Circus acts are carefully choreographed to wow audiences by presenting an array of skills, building from simpler to more daring tricks, planning how the performers will enter and exit the ring and move between tricks, and matching routines precisely to the music. Jessica insists that every act, as well as the entire show, must have a dramatic flow with a beginning, middle, and end, culminating in a spectacle.

The Galilee Arches work on shoulders

Standing behind Ali, Elliana nervously placed her left foot on his left hip. Jessica directed Ali to hold his hands just above his shoulders. She pointed to his right leg to indicate that he should stretch it out behind him. Elliana grasped Ali's hands above her head and hopped her right foot onto his right calf.

"Bend your knees," Jessica ordered him. "Left arm bent. Right arm straight. Now, POWER!"

Together, Jessica and Elliana yanked Ali's arms, forcing him to pull Elliana up. He straightened his right leg and she put her right foot and then her left onto his shoulders. Surprised, he jiggled and she wobbled, but they remained vertical. Pretty soon, half-a-dozen troupers, including Manar, were teetering on someone else's shoulders. Each base tightly clasped the calves of the flyer.

"Juggle? Rolla Bolla?"

Jessica turned to the next task. "Who can juggle?" she shouted. Three Arches and four Galilee kids raised their hands. She told them where to go practice.

"Rolla bolla?" Jessica asked next.

Fortunately, Gilad had taught the Israelis how to balance on a short board laid crosswise atop a cylinder. Roey and Keaton raised their hands. Following Jessica's directions, Roey clambered onto Keaton's shoulders and waited to see what would happen. Keaton stepped onto the board. He shifted and tilted. Roey sat still, his legs clutched around Keaton's torso, trusting that his brand-new friend wouldn't dump him.

Members of both circuses were adept at unicycle, but they were not yet adept at working together. The eight cyclists, including Shai and Kellin, wheeled across the floor, joined hands in pairs, and rolled once around in a circle. "Keep going," Gilad called, swinging his arm in wide circles.

Six other mixed pairs of kids from each circus tried out partner acrobatics. Jessica coached the bases to bend their knees into a deep squat and lean back, their thighs parallel to the floor. To keep from toppling over onto the mat, they reached forward and grasped the thighs of a partner, who stepped onto their knees and leaned forward.

The stance required true partner work because neither the flyer nor the base could hold the position alone, no matter how much experience or strength they had. The acrobats needed each other for balance—a metaphor in circus and in life.

Those on the bottom worried they'd fall over backward. And they did. Those on top fretted that they'd be shoved too far forward or sideways and fall. And, they were. At one time or another, everyone stumbled.

"They Were a Bunch of Kids"

Throughout the rehearsal that afternoon, it seemed to the Americans that the Israelis weren't serious or disciplined. Accustomed to performing every week, the Arches knew how much work was required to stay in shape, to nail their back flips, and to spring high off a mini-tramp, especially a lousy one.

The Galilee kids hadn't even wanted to warm up—a twenty-minute sequence that the Arches followed faithfully before every practice and every show. The Israelis seemed to take frequent breaks, lounging on the mats, chatting, or staring at the Americans. It was as if the Jews and Arabs cared mainly about becoming comfortable with the Americans, while the Americans cared mainly about circus.

"We wanted to focus all the time," Iking said, "and they were a bunch of kids."

In addition to being jet-lagged, many of the Americans were confronting culture shock. Iking, who was already homesick, shook his head, his dreadlocks swinging. "It's so different here." Shaina said, "I didn't know anything about the Israelis." The Arches had expected to team up with other pros, not with amateurs enrolled in a once-a-week after-school program.

After dinner, they all got ready for showtime. As soon as the Galileans saw the Arches' costumes, they snickered. They liked the tight black pants with gold side-stripes, but to them the Arches' gold sleeveless tops, velcroed at the crotch, looked like sparkly golden diapers.

The Israelis didn't like their own shiny, neon-colored, patch-work pants and jackets any better, though. "The costumes were absolutely horrible," Roey admitted. Made of nylon, they were hot to wear and ripped easily.

In a final rehearsal fifteen minutes before curtain, Manar toppled into Jessica's waiting, outstretched arms; she was still unable to balance for long on an Arch's knees or shoulders.

The Galilee Arches warm up

"Ga-li-leeeee Aaaarrr-ches!"

At eight o'clock, just two days after the Arches had left St. Louis, it was time for the troupes to put on their first show. In a corner of the gym, they joined hands, lifted their arms, and belted in unison, "Ga-li-leeeee Aaaarrr-ches!" Jessica admonished them, "No matter what—smile." And, she reminded them, "Remember to style!"

Together, Israelis and Americans pranced onto the gym floor. Together, they smiled even when they dropped balls, rings, diabolos, and each other. With a coach closely spotting each girl, Elliana and Shirel smiled through an unsteady trapeze act. Ali gritted his teeth through some wavery wire walking. For the finale, the twenty-three performers formed a teetering Galilee Arches Pyramid. The audience applauded.

As soon as the show ended, the Israelis sank onto the mats, some of them hugging each other. No one had gotten hurt! Gilad pronounced the show "very good" and gave each of the Americans a T-shirt that read *Kirkas Galil* and *Serk Elgalil*—Galilee Circus, in Hebrew and Arabic, respectively. The T-shirt alternated the two languages.

The Galilee Arches perform a tightwire act

69

"Mazel tov!" Jessica told the group. "Congratulations! You have to clap for yourselves." The Israelis complied, even though they knew they'd been outshone on their own turf. Many of the Americans did not clap. They weren't accustomed to embarrassing themselves in public—and they felt they had. Elliana pronounced the show "very shaky." The two troupes sat apart from each other as they listened to Jessica's recap and pep talk.

"You Are Strange"

Over the weekend, the Americans divided into small groups for homestays in both Jewish and Arab villages. At Roey's house, he, Kellin, and Keaton watched the movie *The Hitchhiker's Guide to the Galaxy* in English, and Roey played "Für Elise" on the piano. At bedtime, Kellin insisted on sleeping on the floor, under Roey's desk, rather than in a bed.

"He scares me," Roey said, partly joking. He even taught Kellin how to say, "You are strange," in Hebrew so Kellin would understand when he said it to him.

Michel and Lemond stayed at Shai's house. One of Shai's neighbors kept some animals, including a camel, in a fenced enclosure. As soon as Lemond saw the camel, he wanted to climb aboard. His host had to explain that this camel was not for riding. Untrained camels can bite.

Shai tried to teach his guests a game called *matkot*. The objective is to keep lobbing a ball back and forth as long as possible. "But [the Americans] thought it was like tennis," he said. "We couldn't convince them that the point is to go on and not make the other person lose."

For the Israelis, the game was collaborative, like circus; for the Americans, it was competitive, like gymnastics. Even though the Americans excelled at performing circus tricks, it was the Israelis who understood that the purpose, at least of *matkot*, was to cooperate.

"I Didn't Feel Comfortable"

Iking, Junior, and other American boys visited Ahmad and his sons, two of whom, Tamer and Saher, were in the circus. The Israelis took the American boys on a tour of their mosque. Iking drew crowds of mystified onlookers, who applauded as he did handsprings and back flips down Deir al-Asad's hilly roads.

The Americans gawked at the dozens of platters of food spread across the table at every meal: Skewers of grilled lamb *shishlik*. Minced lamb *kibbeh* with bulgur wheat. Breaded and fried chicken schnitzel. Pita, *bageli*, and more breads, some sprinkled with olive oil and an herby, sesame-seedy mixture called *za'atar*. The fire-y hot condiment called *zhug*, wrinkled olives, sour pickles. All this food was heaped on their plates by their hosts, whether they wanted it or not.

Shaina yearned for pizza. She was upset that the McDonald's franchises in Israel didn't serve cheeseburgers; many Jews don't mix meat and dairy products for religious reasons. Food imported from America didn't taste right in translation. "I just didn't eat," she said.

Shaina, Elliana, and other female Arches stayed with Manar and Manal. So did Hanni Podlipsky, a Jewish member of the Galilee Circus. She had never slept in an Arab person's home before, nor had the Asadis ever hosted a Jew. Manar and Hanni were gleeful to spend the night together.

The girls watched Manar, who was more observant than her sisters, pray on a special rug that she unfurled on her living room floor. She lifted her hands toward her face, then knelt on the rug and bowed low, her forehead touching the ground. Sitting up, she turned her head to the right and to the left, then recited in Arabic, "Peace and the mercy of God be upon you." Translating the rest of her prayer for her guests, she explained, "I ask my God to make me happy. Make the life easy for me."

Elliana worried about making a mistake that might offend the family. "I'm a nervous wreck," she said. "Am I gonna do the right thing? Am I going to break some custom? It drives me nuts."

Shaina felt the same way. "Being at someone's house, some-one that I didn't know, having to stay with them.... I didn't feel comfortable," she said.

Hala celebrated her tenth birthday that weekend with frosted chocolate layer cake and belly dancing. Everyone clapped and laughed when Elliana danced with Hala and the other Arab girls. Shaina receded into a corner, rather than draw attention to herself.

Ordinarily, the girls would have celebrated Hala's birthday outdoors, on the rooftop of Hala's and Hla's house. But their parents insisted, without explanations, that they stay inside. Neither the Americans nor the Israelis understood why, until the next day.

"There Was a Murder"

First, you should all know that the kids are safe. While the Arches were abroad, Jessica maintained a blog for the folks back home. This worrisome statement opened the second paragraph of her post on July 15, 2007. The next sentence was chilling.

There was a murder in the Arab village last night.

On the evening of Hala's birthday, a member of their family's clan, the Asadi, was murdered by a member of another clan, the Musa. The killer was captured and jailed. By local custom, his ten brothers and their families were also banished from Deir al-Asad. They had to leave within twenty-four hours or risk being killed in revenge. The crime also spurred rioting, and the perpetrator's home, which was only two houses away from Ahmad's, was burned, along with his family's automobiles.

For their own protection, the girls were kept indoors. The American and Arab boys ventured to Ahmad's rooftop. From there, they could see the victim's relatives carrying his cloth-wrapped body through the streets, followed by about a thousand fellow Asadis, many of them holding flaming torches.

Iking might have been troubled by reminders of his uncle's murder the previous year. Or by the parallels between the clan

72

violence in Deir al-Asad and the gang violence in St. Louis. So many of his close friends had been shot and killed that he had just about lost count. Instead, Iking blithely commented, "We see stuff like this all the time."

"They Kept Coming and Coming"

Because of the rioting and fires in Deir al-Asad, the two circuses couldn't perform their first public show there the next day. Marc quickly found another gym in the nearby Arab town of Majd al-Krum. Everybody worried that no one would show up. And when they saw the gym, they almost hoped no one would: it was not only smaller than the one in Deir al-Asad, but it was also infested with pigeons. To attract an audience, a man who owned a watermelon-delivery truck equipped with a loudspeaker drove through the villages, announcing the new location. And Jessica dismissed the pigeon infestation with, "If they poop on you, it's good luck."

Throngs of Arab villagers streamed into the gym. "They kept coming and coming and coming," Jessica said. By showtime, about 500 people crammed the bleachers or sat cross-legged on the floor. For the Galilee kids, who performed only three times a year in front of their parents and friends, the crowd seemed daunting. Even the Arches were stunned.

Shaina hoped to do her usual trapeze act, but because this was the Arabs' hometown crowd, Jessica asked her if Manar could perform instead. Reluctantly but graciously, Shaina agreed, even though that meant she'd have a smaller role in the show.

Manar was still afraid of the trapeze, so Jessica stood next to her to support and spot her in case she got into trouble. Manar could barely do a simple Bird's Nest, but she managed to hang upside down by her knees. She beamed proudly when she landed safely on the mat.

Manar Asadi debuts on the trapeze

Despite Gilad's training, Roey kept slipping off his rolla bolla, partly because the boxes he'd stacked on the cylinder were bloated from the heat. Keaton rolled side to side on his board, waiting to start their act. When Roey finally found his balance, the crowd clapped and cheered for him.

Yaron and Noam passed nine balls. "At the Arches," Kellin realized, "we were not even close to that level of juggling." But assuming that the trick wasn't really that difficult, he remained unimpressed by the Galilee Circus's overall ability. "I could do that," he thought with cocky self-assurance. "That wouldn't be hard."

Later that night, Deon White, Matt, and Junior displayed their brand-new staff-twirling skills—complete with fire—at an after-show party. Roey said they performed better than the more-experienced Israelis. Shai reminded him that it wasn't supposed to be a competition.

Tefillin and *Fajr*

The Galilee Arches hit the road the next day to visit historic, religious, and nature sites around the country. Along the way, the kids played, bickered, performed, and—with the exception of Shaina—became friends.

Buoyed by the high salt content, they floated effortlessly in the Dead Sea. Almost ten times saltier than the ocean, the water felt slimy on their skin. They performed in Tel Aviv along the boardwalk that skirts that section of the Mediterranean Sea shoreline—nearly slipping in their own sweat. They spotted jackals during a nighttime jeep trip in the mountainous Golan Heights—and grumbled about their sore bottoms from the bumpy ride. They slept on pallets inside a Bedouin tent in the barren, rocky Negev Desert and—except for Kellin, who thought it was exotic, and Shaina, who took it in stride—whined about the lack of electricity, running water, and indoor toilets.

Early one morning, under a canvas canopy that protected them from the already-searing sun at their Bedouin campsite, Marc placed a prayer shawl called a *tallit* around his shoulders, on top of his T-shirt. Then he "lay *tefillin*": he wrapped a narrow leather strap around his forehead and wound another one round and

Fire poi on the beach

round his right arm, hand, and middle finger. The straps ended in a tiny leather box that contained a Biblical commandment written on parchment. The commandment, he explained, directs Jews to remember the exodus from Egypt and to "bind these words as a sign upon your hand and put them as a sign between your eyes." Then, he prayed, rocking slightly back and forth.

The Galilee Arches relax in a Bedouin tent

As he finished reading from the Jewish prayer book, Manar joined him under the canopy for the morning Muslim prayer called *Fajr*. She removed her shoes and pulled a long white skirt over her black leggings. Then she repeated the prayers that the girls had watched her recite at home.

Lemond rides a camel

In the Old City in Jerusalem, the Galilee Arches gazed at the silver-domed Al-Aqsa Mosque in the Muslim Quarter. They whispered in the Church of the Holy Sepulcher in the Christian Quarter, slipped handwritten prayers into chinks in the Western Wall in the Jewish Quarter, and strolled past the St. James Monastery in the Armenian Quarter. In addition, Lemond finally got his chance to ride a camel!

When the Americans stayed in Deir al-Asad, they saw only Arabs. When they stayed in Karmiel or Atzmon, they saw only Jews. Traveling in other parts of Israel, they saw both Arabs and

Jews on the streets but they were not walking together.

One of the Arches noticed, "It was just Arab people walking together and, then, Jews walking together.... There was more differences [between Arabs and Jews] than blacks and whites." Seeing the separate villages and the separate social groups, T-Roc concluded that Israel was even more segregated than St. Louis.

Shaina found this to be the case within the Galilee Circus as well. "The Arabs and Jews separated themselves from each other, unless they needed to be together," she observed. On the streets and in shops, Shaina said, "Jews and Arabs didn't treat each other nicely." Armed soldiers patrolled everywhere—along sidewalks, at entrances to museums, and in the *shuk*, the market where she bought a belly-dancing outfit. When the Americans saw a Jewish shopkeeper kick an Arab boy out of his shop, they put down the items they'd intended to buy and walked out in protest.

"I Was Fighting with Her"

It wasn't just strangers who sometimes treated each other badly. In a tense exchange one hot and exhausting day, Shirel, who was Jewish, called Ali "a stinking Arab." Angry, Ali walked away.

An even more unpleasant clash arose when Hanni was injured during a performance near the Dead Sea. She cried, and Ali told her to shut up. He warned other performers standing nearby, "I will slap her, if needed. Make her go blind." As he moved a tightwire apparatus, Hanni shouted at him, "Just so it will fall on your head, and you will die!"

In a mixture of Arabic and Hebrew, they continued to yell at each other. "I was fighting with her since we started the circus," Ali said. "There are some girls here that do not respect themselves much—and need beating."

The notion of beating a girl as punishment for speaking back to a boy would have stunned the Americans, had they understood. The Israelis, on the other hand, were not surprised to hear two tense and tired circus performers, one of whom happened to be

Arab and the other Jewish, quarrel nastily. They were also familiar with an Arab male's perspective that a female should keep quiet.

At one point Shai and Jessica faced off. "I misplaced my pants I was supposed to wear in a show," Shai said. "Jessica was yelling at me. And I was upset with her. I refused to go in the show." Shai understood that he was responsible for keeping track of his pants but he didn't want to be yelled at.

"Fire. Inside. Near Children."

Many shows remained, as Keaton declared, "unfocused, sloppy, and messed up." But the Galilee Arches managed to clean up some of their acts.

They performed for three hundred enthusiastic day campers at the Young Men's Christian Association in Jerusalem. Shai and Keaton unicycled together. Roey hopped effortlessly onto a rolla bolla, while Keaton haphazardly slid right off of his. Manar lifted her leg, unaided, over the trapeze bar and styled.

"And, now, for the first time ever," Jessica announced at the finale, "Fire. Inside. Near children."

The gym's lights dimmed and Shai and Deon came out swinging fire staff, followed by Mysa and Lemond with fire poi.

After the show, campers swarmed the performers to shake their hands and try to talk with them. Surrounded by small admirers, Iking said, "I guess they love me."

"The Total Obliteration of Barriers"

"For me," Jessica said, "the defining moment was the show we did at Bet Kessler, the home for people with cerebral palsy. It brought me back to the first traveling youth circus I was a part of, The Circus Kingdom.... To be in the circus is to give. It is not the tricks you do. It is what you give—to those you perform with and to your audience. It was the moment that these children, together, gave this gift of themselves to the people at Bet Kessler."

Watching the Galilee Arches perform, Jessica realized, "I'm keeping on the legacy." She was giving back, as she had promised Warren, fulfilling her mission.

Keaton and Shai perform their unicycle act

For Marc, the experiences had accumulated. "I think many who saw the shows felt the same tears in their eyes, maybe out of the feeling one is seeing a vision of something that we all long for…the total obliteration of barriers, whether social, economic, or gravitational."

At the farewell gathering Kellin belly danced with a spangly scarf knotted around his hips. "I think the Israeli kids should come and visit our circus in America," he said.

He wasn't sad to leave, though. "I kind of miss the people at home," he admitted, even though he'd been traveling with his mother and siblings. He wanted to sleep in his own bed, rather than in a Bedouin tent or under Roey's desk. Iking, too, yearned to return home, even though his home was one of the most difficult to return to.

"Go in Peace"

The next day, the Galilee Circus trooped to the airport to wish the St. Louis Arches bon voyage. The Israelis presented the Americans with a balancing ladder, juggling staffs, Galilee wine, and four pots of mint, which U.S. Customs did not allow them to carry aboard. No one did acrobatics, as Alex and Junior had two weeks earlier. But many hugged their new friends and cried.

Shai couldn't understand why the kids were sad. "It was so obvious to me that we're going to meet them again," he said.

Shaina didn't cry either. "I hadn't connected with the girls as well as everyone else did," she said. "So, I wasn't too sad about leaving." In any case, she'd be returning to Illinois soon. Even if the Galilee Circus did manage to come to America, she probably wouldn't see them again.

Marc offered a traditional farewell in Arabic and Hebrew:

Ma'assalama   مع السلامة
Tzehu le Shalom   צאו לשלום
Go in peace

Keaton and Roey juggle on rolla bollas at Bet Kessler

79

Jessica shared the customary circus farewell: "See you down the road."

The St. Louis Arches had learned to overlook the Galileans' gaffes, communicate without a common language, and appreciate some new friendships. Iking was now aware that many worlds exist outside of central St. Louis. Early in the trip, he had asked Marc, "How am I supposed to tell the Arabs from the Jews?" By the end, he understood why Marc had answered, "You're not."

The Galilee Circus, having finally seen a real circus in action, had become aware of how much they could improve. "We came there to have fun," Roey said. "We didn't care about the performance; we didn't take it seriously. Only after meeting the Arches, we started taking ourselves seriously. We got really motivated after that."

Chapter Six

AMERICA? 2007–2008

B y the time the kids split off and headed back home, it was hard to know which troupe was more astonished—the St. Louis Arches, none of whom had ever stepped outside the continental U.S., or the Galilee Circus kids, none of whom had ever attempted so many new tricks in such a short time.

Their confrontations with and sharing of each other's cultures, practices, and assumptions had given everyone new insights. Elliana found Israelis to be more exuberant than Americans. "We were all very reserved," she said, "while the Israelis were much more outgoing." On the other hand, Kellin agreed with Shaina, who realized, "they were no different than us."

The circus kids' impressions and experiences were revelations. They returned home—whether to St. Louis, Rock Island, Karmiel, Atzmon, or Deir al-Asad—with wider eyes and bigger ambitions.

"I Want to Do That Too"

Now that they were aware of what a youth circus could look like, some of the Israelis yearned to become more professional. Roey put it this way: "The only thing we thought about was 'I want to do that too.'"

"We can still be friends, but we need to be professional."

—Shirel Mondrik

Road sign for Karmiel

Jewish Holidays in the Fall

A string of Jewish holidays occurs over about three weeks every fall. Rosh Hashanah celebrates New Year's. A ten-day period of repentance ends on Yom Kippur, when Jews fast and ask God and each other for forgiveness. During Sukkot, a weeklong harvest festival, they eat outdoors in decorated huts. On Shemini Atzeret, they pray for rain. Simchat Torah celebrates the end of the weekly readings from the Torah, the first five books of the Bible.

As it turned out, though, their ambitions had to be set aside. The Jewish holidays fell later than usual in 2007, which meant that Jewish schools were closed and the circus would have to wait until they opened.

Coincidentally, the Muslim month of Ramadan, which can occur throughout the year, started in mid-September as well. Israeli school and circus calendars don't take it into consideration, so having the time off was unusual for the Arab performers. Like all practicing Muslims, many fasted during the month, and they were relieved that they didn't have to practice on empty stomachs.

Finally, mid-October arrived and circus began again. The break hadn't dulled their ambitions. Just about everyone started or returned to circus that fall with a vision.

On her first day, Hla strode in with a plan. She had seen contortionists perform on television and was entranced. She showed YouTube videos to Leonid Tzipkis, a coach who specialized in gymnastics and contortion. "I want to do that," she told him.

Hala had her eye on aerials. Thanks to the Arches, the Galilee Circus now had a trapeze. Hala hadn't seen any of their joint shows during the summer, but Manar had told her about them. Manar said that although she'd found the trapeze hard at first, she'd liked some of the easier tricks. Even though she'd felt awkward, she told Hala that she was proud of learning to do a routine by herself.

Shai wanted to improve his toss juggling. He also wanted to try out an act using staffs with Noam.

Roey vowed to learn to handle three diabolos—a much harder skill than juggling just two of them. "Your movements have to be faster…," he said, "The eye-hand coordination is a lot harder.… In two diabolos, if the diabolos have enough speed, they can just go on without [you] needing to do anything with your hands.… If you do nothing with your hands, the three diabolos will just drop." He understood the problems, but he wasn't sure how to fix them.

Roey also wanted to learn acrobatics. The only tumbling tricks anyone at the Galilee Circus could manage were forward and backward rolls on the floor. Thinking of Iking's soaring back tucks, Roey realized that rolls hardly counted.

Mostly, what the Galilee Circus kids wanted to do was whatever the Arches did. Roey and Shai, along with Shirel, Yaron, and Noam, clamored for their circus to become more serious.

"Some of Them Were Kind of…Lazy"

They all had goals. Meeting them would be a challenge. Eager to try out their new trapeze, Leonid, Gilad, and Amit sought out an aerials coach. They found Dagan Dishbak, who had helped found Israel's first trapeze school.

Dagan had no experience working with children, but the offer appealed to him. "It was more meaningful," he realized, "not only kids but different kinds of kids working together, Jewish and Arab." Attracted by the opportunity to work on behalf of Arab-Jewish coexistence, he decided to try training young people.

Soon after joining the staff as head coach, he noticed that the physical conditioning of many of the Galilee Circus kids was, as he tactfully put it, "not so high." To be frank, he added, "some of them were kind of heavy or, maybe, lazy." If they really wanted to become professional, they had a lot of work to do.

The performers had other problems too. While many of them were pretty good at their specialty, they didn't do a variety of tricks. Shirel had learned some tightwire, but not much else. Jugglers like Roey and Shai were competent with diabolo and balls, but lacked experience with clubs. The Arab boys mostly did acro.

"We Need to Be Professional"

So Dagan introduced a major change. Warm-ups ballooned from five minutes of trotting around the gym and shaking out their arms to thirty minutes of intensive jumping, running, resistance

Ramadan and *Eid Al-Fitr*

During the month of Ramadan, which is the ninth month of the Islamic lunar calendar, Muslims fast from dawn until sunset and are encouraged to recite the entire Qur'an. Each day's fasting ends with a festive meal, called the *iftar*. Toward the end of the month, the holiest night of the year recalls the night when, Muslims believe, the Qur'an was revealed to Mohammed. The holiday *Eid al-Fitr* celebrates the end of Ramadan and the beginning of the new month.

An amateur athlete, **Dagan Dishbak** attended a small, informal circus school in Florida after he finished his mandatory army service. He became entranced with circus but discovered that there was neither a circus nor a circus school in Israel. To further his training, he traveled to Turkey, the United States, Brazil, and other countries.

The first time he tried flying trapeze, he felt the same way Alex did. "I fell in love," he said. "It was a bit crazy because not many people do it…. For me, I felt more happy up there. It felt natural."

exercises, and stretching. The kids who wanted to get serious about circus huffed, puffed, and staggered through the warm-ups as best as they could. Those who didn't made faces. Some openly grumbled. When Dagan introduced cross training for a variety of skills, the complaints escalated.

Dagan noticed that it was mostly the Arab kids who resisted his demands. "They're paying less attention than the Jewish kids," he said. "The Jewish kids are more critical about themselves. They demand more from themselves. The Arab kids don't focus on perfect performance. They say, 'Yeah, whatever.'"

Many of the Arabs were satisfied with their circus as it was. They didn't feel a need to be pushed. Many of the Jews, on the other hand, wanted to transform the Galilee into a real circus. They felt frustrated that the Arabs seemed more interested in remaining a relaxed and friendly after-school activity. "We can still be friends," Shirel insisted, "but we need to be professional." The Jewish kids didn't understand that the gym was the only place where Arab kids could hang out together.

The Arabs and Jews agreed on at least one issue, though. Everyone got exasperated with Shai. "When I or someone else is saying something, he always has something else to say," Dagan complained. He mimicked Shai: "'Why is it like that? I think it should be the opposite.'"

Then Shai would grumble that Dagan lost his patience and yelled at him "for no reason."

"Shai is a difficult guy," Dagan said.

"You Have to Do It"

Tensions seemed to increase as expectations rose. Nevertheless, Dagan insisted that everyone participate. "It's important," he told them, "to make you stronger and more flexible, in good shape for the future. Even if it's hard now, even if you don't like it, you have to do it…. This is part of the class."

Dagan got almost everyone up on the trapeze, at least a few times. Hala, Hla, and Shirel loved it. Amit and Gilad coached juggling, tightwire, and stilts walking as well as basic acrobatics, including that Arches staple—Pyramids. The Galilee kids also had to work on their mini-tramp skills—still using the same lifeless equipment and the flat, horsehair mattresses.

Coaching had also become a source of frustration—and not just for Shai. When Marc visited a practice session one evening, he saw a girl hanging from a trapeze with no spotter nearby. "Pay attention!" he warned Dagan. Marc wondered if the kids were safe with Dagan in charge.

The Galilee coaches were more casual, less attentive than those who worked with the Arches. They demonstrated how a trick should be done and then let the young performers work on their own to try to develop the skill. But the previous summer, Marc had seen how the Arches' coaches had been literally hands-on. They didn't just show tricks; they physically bent, stretched, and lifted the troupers' bodies into, through, and out of the tricks. That way, the youngsters could feel, not just see, how to do them.

Circus, whether it involved professionals or kids, was young in this relatively new country. And the techniques to train performers were still developing.

"I Have to Learn This Trick"

Another difference separated the Israelis and the Americans: the number of opportunities to perform. The Arches, who performed year-round week after week, often for paying audiences, were truly professionals. The Galilee Circus, which staged shows for parents and close friends at the end of the year, was composed of amateurs. It was a circus in name only.

Marc and the Israeli coaches decided to aim higher. They sought opportunities for the Galilee Circus to display what they were learning. When a few facilities for disabled children invited them to perform, they knew they had to hone their presentation.

One step toward more a more professional presentation in-volved upgrading their costumes from the patchwork outfits they had worn the previous summer to gold tops with black pants, like those worn by the Arches. Fortunately, without a velcro closure at the groin, they didn't look like golden diapers. Shai liked the new costumes, though Roey thought they looked weird.

More importantly, the Galilee Circus needed to display more finesse. The coaches told them to stand erect with their arms behind their backs while their partners performed, and to style when they completed a trick.

The Israeli troupers began to pine for another visit—not for the Arches to return to Israel, but for the Galilee Circus to travel to America. "Every time we started to learn a new trick," Roey said, "we told ourselves, 'I have to learn this trick [before] we come to the U.S.' That was a motivation—coming to [see] the Arches."

Even if they had no idea if such a venture was possible.

"All Circus, All the Time"

A day after the Arches returned from Israel, most of them turned around and flew to Nantucket, an island off the coast of Massachusetts, to perform with Circus Flora. Neither Shaina nor Iking went along. Shaina had to return to Rock Island. And Iking, who had become desperately homesick during his two weeks in Israel, couldn't bear to leave St. Louis again.

Jessica implored him. She felt he had an obligation to the Arches. But Iking refused. After performing in a few shows that fall, he told her he wanted to drop out of circus. "We were told to be adults," he said. "We were supposed to mature at a very young age, to perform as circus artists. Jessica put so much pressure on us." He planned to keep in touch with his circus friends by selling popcorn and soft drinks at their shows.

Diane hoped he'd stick with the program, but she was no more persuasive than Jessica. "She let me make choices," Iking said, "and I had to live with them if they were bad."

At home, Iking had few good examples to follow. His oldest brother had been badly injured in an accident in a stolen car and

Wearing the Galilee Circus's new costume, Shai juggles on the globe

was "messed up in his head." Once he tried to choke Iking. His other brothers were in and out of jail. Fortunately, he realized, "They wasn't doing anything productive that I pictured myself doing."

The only family member he admired was Cat. "My sister was my role model," he said. Because she played school sports, Iking decided he would too.

"I didn't want to do all circus, all the time," he said. "I was too young to devote myself to circus. I always wanted to play basketball and football." In fact, he hoped to become a professional basketball player, even though he wasn't nearly as tall or lean as most pro players.

But when the football season ended, he got bored. "So it was basically an off-and-on thing with circus and football. I tried to juggle these three things around—high school, high school sports, and circus." Iking and Jessica lost track of the number of times he dropped in and out of circus.

"Show the Circus World What We've Got"

In the fall, the Arches encountered a situation that was new to them—something similar to what the Galilee Circus kids had experienced when they watched the Arches hurl themselves into the air at Kibbutz Sasa.

During their Ringling performance, the Arches noticed another group of young people, also in costumes, gathered nearby. At the end of their act, the Arches watched this other youth circus perform. "We were completely blown out of the water," Rosie Eastman, an Arch, said. "They were doing these incredible tricks, ones that seemed impossible."

Instead of being intimidated, the Arches were motivated. The Windy City Acrobats, Rosie said, "inspired us to do bigger, better things.... Every single one of us is ready to show the circus world what we've got."

87

"Not Giving Up"

In January 2008, Jessica contacted Marc. Would the Galilee Circus like to come to St. Louis this summer? Maybe, he answered, as long as arrangements, especially fund-raising, could be made quickly. The U.S. government required every Israeli citizen to have a visa to enter the country, and everyone over the age of fourteen would have to be interviewed individually by a U.S. embassy staff member in Tel Aviv. Obtaining visas, especially for the Arab children, could take months.

In February, Jessica had to explain to Marc that Circus Harmony's board of directors had told her they couldn't raise the funds necessary for an international trip every year. They weren't prepared to donate, beg, and scrounge for a second year in a row.

Jessica decided to proceed anyway. She proposed that the Galilee Circus come to St. Louis in early July. She asked Marc to draw up a budget so the board would know exactly how much money they'd need to raise. With her typical determination, she signed her message, "Not giving up."

Marc responded, "We continue to have our doubts, despite your enthusiasm."

His doubts included not only the "money problem" but also concerns about the Galilee Circus kids' skills. He just didn't think they were solid enough to justify a trip across the world. Dagan was getting mixed evaluations, so Marc knew he might have to search for a new head coach. More importantly, the dates Jessica had proposed wouldn't work. A teacher strike in Israel had shut down the schools, which had only recently reopened, and they wouldn't close for the year until mid-July. There were just too many obstacles. Maybe the Galilee Circus could come to St. Louis another year.

No more discouraged by Marc's concerns than she was by her board's reservations, Jessica continued to confront the logistical barriers to a visit from the Israelis. Perhaps a hotel or her husband's business or City Museum would donate rooms? Might Whole Foods contribute meals? Would a Jewish organization pay for the

Israelis' airfare? What if she could arrange an appearance on *The Oprah Winfrey Show*? And could she make all of these decisions and arrangements while running a youth circus in a city that was suddenly inundated by the flooding waters of the Mississippi River?

In addition, there was the matter of the tricks that the Galilee Circus could perform with the Arches. Had they started tumbling? she asked Marc. Tried out the trapeze or the globe the Arches had given them last year? Jessica began communicating with Dagan about programming.

Keenly aware of the many hindrances to such a trip, Marc was less committed to it than Jessica. He didn't say anything to the Galilee Circus kids about it. Instead, he concentrated on helping Dagan improve his management skills. And all of the kids needed to upgrade their tumbling, acrobatics, wire walking, aerials, juggling, flexibility, strength, discipline, and general performance skills. Maybe they'd be ready by next year.

"We Tried…"

Throughout the spring, "everybody took everything more seriously," Roey said. "Every time we had a show, we tried to make it more professional. We started practicing acrobatics and juggling more."

Roey especially wanted to achieve his vow of manipulating three diabolos, so he practiced every day, gradually getting better and better. "I started teaching myself new tricks by watching videos on YouTube and talking to other jugglers online in all sorts of juggling forums…. I learned everything by myself."

But Roey still couldn't manage three diabolos. If only he could, then he could add more impressive tricks to his routine, such as tossing and rotating them in the air. But whenever he tried, one or two would bounce off and roll away.

Shai and Noam worked up a kung-fu staff-twirling routine. "It was like a battle to the death," Shai explained. "We looked at each other, looked at the audience, and looked at each other. We were pointing [staffs]...and running toward each other like a fight. I would roll on his back. I swung my staff under him, and he would jump over it. Then, we'd switch.... It was a very good act. We worked on it for the entire year."

In June, the Galilee Circus held its one-night, end-of-year show for the kids' families. The performers gathered in a circle behind the star-spangled paper screen propped up on the gym floor, stacked their hands, and then lifted them in unison. They had learned this team gesture from the Arches, who had begun every show last summer with "Galilee Arches!" This time, they shouted, *"Kirkas Galil!"*

They performed their best tricks. Roey juggled two diabolos and spun one along the string under his leg. Hala and Hla stretched into splits and back bends and did forward and backward rolls. Shai and Noam tossed a flower stick back and forth, while Shai sat on Noam's shoulders and Noam balanced on a rolla bolla. Shai was disappointed, though, that his partner refused to do their kung-fu act.

They knew the show was rudimentary, especially in comparison with the high-level tricks they'd seen the Arches do the year before.

On-Again, Off-Again

Meghan was now an intermediate-level circus trainee. She found herself becoming more and more drawn to circus. In particular, she was entranced by a young contortionist, Mei Ling Robin, who could pull off amazing stunts like doing vertical splits while standing on one foot in another performer's hands. "It was awesome," Meghan said. "I loved watching her work."

Junior was teaching a class in flexibility, and he noticed Meghan's growing interest and improved abilities. He told her about the class and said, "You need to come."

Without knowing exactly what it would entail, Meghan agreed. "Junior started pulling out me and Max," Meghan said, referring to another student, "and working with us privately...

Shai and Noam perform flower sticks on the rolla bolla

pushing us to work, making circus more serious. He was the one who started me training in contortion."

Iking was not having such a successful year. Sports kept him occupied during the fall but they ended in the spring, and he hadn't rejoined circus. "I had time on my hands," he said, "so I got into trouble."

He skipped class to shoot baskets in the gym. He punched out other kids and was suspended from school. "I needed some extra activities to do to keep me on the right track because when basketball season was over, there's nothing else for me to do but goof off and have fun."

Circus was an on-again, mostly off-again, thing for him. His grandmother couldn't handle him. Diane couldn't persuade him to return to circus. He hadn't stolen cars like his brothers or gotten into drugs, but the people who cared about him feared that he might.

An Israeli trip to America also seemed on-again, off-again. Marc pressed Jessica for a decision in May. "We have to start applying for visas now," he explained. "We don't want to be in a situation in which they go through this effort and expense for naught. I need for you to say 'yes, go ahead.'" But, Jessica couldn't say, "Yes." And she didn't want to say, "No."

"Exquisite Combination of People and Talent"

At about the same time as the Galilee end-of-year show, the Arches performed for three weeks under the Circus Flora tent. Shaina returned from Rock Island just in time to tumble out with the troupe.

Although she hadn't rehearsed circus routines since last summer, Shaina was still in good form. She was becoming a track star at her school, running the 50- and 100-meter dashes, as well as the 4 x 100 hundred relay, in which she served as her team's anchor across the finish line. She had even started winning some ribbons.

Shaina had also joined the cheerleading team where she was the star tumbler. Actually she was their *only* tumbler. "When

Junior performs a hand stand on stacked chairs

91

The Arches at Circus Flora
In front: Shaina, Kellin,
Keaton, Lil Donald
In back: Matthias Staley, Lemond,
Alex, Elliana, Matt, Claire, Junior,
Anthony, Iking

I tumbled," she said, "the crowd went wild. It was like circus but not circus." Her coach was strict but Shaina was used to high expectations.

At Jessica's request, Iking rejoined the troupe to sub for an Arch who had hurt his back in a rehearsal. Jessica assumed that Iking was back for good; Shaina wished that she could stay too.

A dozen Arches joined Circus Flora for the production. Even without much recent practice, Iking flipped and flung himself into double-twisting and double-tuck somersaults. The voltige crew debuted new maneuvers on horseback. Shaina whipped through so many back flips that a reviewer for *The St. Louis American* gushed, "she seemed to be spinning 360 degrees in a circle that appeared to lift four inches from the ground. Thirteen-year-old Shaina Hughes seemed to defy gravity."

In a newsletter, Jessica described their Circus Flora presentation as "the end of an Arches era.… [T]his exquisite combination of people and talent has achieved more than any group before." Two of the Arches were heading to top-notch circus programs—one at Florida State University and the other in Canada.

Then Iking announced that he was abandoning circus yet again, this time to play basketball. Jessica mourned, "We have never lost so many at the same time." She worried most about Iking and asked Marc to pray for him. "His situation is the most difficult of any kid I have dealt with."

"Maybe, Maybe"

During the spring and early summer, Jessica managed to solicit—though not yet collect—donations for the Galilee Circus troupe's airfare and schedule the trip so it wouldn't conflict with the Israelis' school calendar. Marc finally decided it was time to tell the kids that they might be going to America.

But which kids? Marc and the coaches conferred. They agreed on Manar and Manal; Hala and Hla were too young and inexperienced to make the trip. They also chose Mysa, Tamer, Yaron, Noam, Roey, Ali, Shirel, Shai, and Dana Raz.

Saher had hoped to go to St. Louis, but he had slipped off a mat and broken his kneecap earlier in June. Instead, Ahmed Asadi (who was not related to Hala or Hla) took his place. Marc wondered about the choice. Unlike the other Arab children in the group, Ahmed spoke little Hebrew and no English, and he seemed to have serious learning disabilities. But Marc figured the coaches knew best.

The troupe would consist of six boys and six girls, half of them Arab and half Jewish. Of course, Marc and Dagan would also go. When Roey's mother learned that no women were accompanying the group, she volunteered to help oversee the girls.

This cast was still theoretical, though. No one knew if the trip was definitely going to happen. "We knew we were going there," Shai said. "We just didn't know for sure because they kept telling us 'Maybe, maybe. It depends on how much money we can gather.'"

Near the end of June—just five weeks before their departure—Jessica was still working on finding housing, funds for side trips, and money for everyone's meals. Meanwhile, she asked Marc if he could send graphics for T-shirts reading *Galilee Arches USA 2008* and *Peace through Pyramids* in all three alphabets: Arabic, English, and Hebrew.

But Marc was far from ready to design T-shirts. He still needed a firm decision about whether the trip was on or off. If it was on, he also needed a detailed itinerary. He wrote Jessica.

> *We have a parent meeting on Sunday; can you send us any further information about the schedule, housing etc.? The Ministry of Education is also on our case, as they have to approve all foreign trips of kids, and they are nagging for info on schedule and accommodations.*

With so many logistics up in the air, Jessica still couldn't commit. She said she could send an itinerary but, at that point, it would be a "fantasy." To urge the U. S. embassy to grant the visas, she wrote a letter to the American ambassador to Israel.

> *Last summer, eleven American children from different socioeconomic and religious backgrounds went to Israel where they worked together with a group of thirteen Israeli Jewish and Arab children… When you see them together,*

you are struck by their abilities—their abilities to juggle, balance and fly through the air: but more importantly, you are struck by their abilities to trust, to work together and to give to others. The Galilee Arches flew together physically, emotionally, socially and spiritually. The Galilee Arches showed the true meaning of trust, courage and team-work. These daring young circus performers embodied the concept of social circus: using circus arts to motivate social change... For the summer of 2008, we want to show Americans what over 2000 people witnessed last year in Israel.

The letter persuaded the ambassador that this unlikely mixture of Arab and Jewish circus performers was legitimate, and he approved the trip. It was time to apply for visas for everyone. After driving from the Galilee to Tel Aviv, the Galilee Circus troupers had to wait at the embassy. "There was a huge line that day," Shai said, "and we had to stand the entire time." He and Noam made a bet on how long it would take; Shai lost. After seven hours, they finally got their visas for America. All they needed were places to stay, food to eat, and everything else Jessica was trying to corral.

95

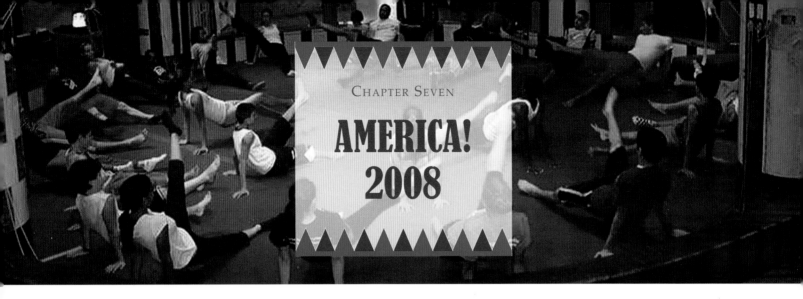

N ear the end of June, Marc was finally able to tell the dozen selected troupers that they would be leaving for St. Louis on July 30. "We're going to America!" Shai exclaimed. "*Sababa!*" This is the Arabic word that many Israelis, whether Arabic or Hebrew speakers, use for "Awesome!"

None of the Arab kids had ever traveled that far, though some of the Jewish kids had. Roey had visited relatives in Canada; Shai had traveled to England and Greece. Shirel had also traveled abroad. Most of the others had never even been on an airplane.

To young people growing up in a miniscule country where some of their ancestors might have lived for the past half-millennium, the expansiveness and newness of America were alluring. Besides, they had friends there—circus friends.

"What Is the Purpose of Your Travel?"

"Me and a few other kids from the circus decided that, by the time we meet the Arches again in 2008, we'll each make progress and learn new things," Roey said.

The Galilee Circus didn't meet in July. Outside of circus, the Jews and Arabs never saw each other, so they couldn't practice the basic partner acrobatics that they had been learning. Those who could, practiced alone at home.

> "Not everybody fits the same mold. That keeps it interesting."
>
> —Sariya Saabye

The Galilee Arches warm up in the Circus Harmony ring

A week before they left for the U.S., the travelers gathered at Marc's office. They were excited to see each other and ready to prepare for their trip.

Dagan brought out pairs of heavy wooden planks, each over six feet long. Half a dozen short rope loops were attached to each board, evenly spaced along the top. He divided the kids into mixed teams and gave each group a pair of planks and an assignment: get from one side of the space to the other—without touching the ground.

It wasn't long before they figured out how to do it. Place two boards parallel. Have everybody on a team line up, one person behind another. Each person places a foot in a loop on each board. Then everyone simultaneously shuffles forward, left-right, left-right. Shai thought the game was silly, because he felt they were already a team, but he still had fun.

Then Dagan went over the rules of travel: Stay with the group. Watch your belongings. They discussed what clothes to bring; the Midwest summer would be less hot but more humid than the Galilee.

Marc packed a large-format photograph of last year's combined Galilee Arches. Roey's mother brought one of her pottery statuettes for Jessica. Several kids took along gifts for their American friends, including Shai, who had found a stuffed camel for Lemond.

Because they would be a travel party of both Arabs and Jews—a suspect mix—Marc alerted airport officials in advance. Security and background checks there can be extensive. He told the kids that examiners would ask them questions: "What is the purpose of your travel?" "Did you pack your own suitcase?" "Has anyone given you anything to carry on the plane?"

Worried that Ahmed wouldn't understand the questions, the troupers worked together to prepare him. At the airport they were escorted courteously through the checkpoint, thanks to Marc's advance call. The kids thought that preparing Ahmed had been unnecessary—until officials confronted him during a stop-over in Turkey. Ahmed repeated the answers they'd taught him: "Circus." "Yes." "No." Fortunately, the security officer asked him the questions in the order they'd predicted, and they all breezed through the checkpoint.

"It's Like Living in the Circus"

Manar and Manal had never been on a plane before. At first they'd been scared, but then Manar realized, "On the trapeze, I have self-confidence…. The airplane was like a big trapeze."

Thirty hours later, they finally landed in St. Louis. "When we got out," Roey said, "the Arches were waiting for us with signs and making lots of noise. Everybody was really excited."

Kellin clambered onto Noam's shoulders and juggled balls while Noam searched for his suitcase.

Roey was especially eager to see Iking. He had something to tell him. But to his disappointment, he discovered that Iking had dropped out of circus.

Everyone piled into a rented yellow school bus, and Jessica drove them straight to City Museum. The Israelis were startled and confused to discover that the Arches practiced and performed in a museum—especially such a bizarre one. "It was weird," Shai said.

The girls and most of the boys would stay in lofts in the building; the other boys would stay in an apartment across the street. "It's like living in the circus," Marc observed. Exhausted, the kids and adults tumbled into bed.

Early the next the morning, Ali and Dagan explored the museum before it opened to the public. "It was scary and funny and weird," Dagan said. "It looks like a big maze when you first get there…. I love this place!"

Jessica did not make allowances for jet lag. She put an end to the exploration, called the Galilee Arches to order, and introduced the visitors to the facilities at Circus Harmony.

The Israelis immediately discovered the advantages of hav-

Kellin juggles while sitting on Noam's shoulders at the St. Louis airport

ing a space dedicated to circus. A real ring. Stage lighting. Permanent rigging. Built-in seats. A backstage classroom with mats and equipment that didn't have to be hauled out of closets before every class. A chute to line up in, offstage. A separate room for trapeze and tightwire practice. Boys' and girls' dressing rooms.

And they didn't have to share their space with an entire community. Maybe someday, the Israelis thought hopefully, the Galilee Circus will also have its own facility.

"Mishma'at!"

The troupers had lengthy warm-ups to do, tricks to share, and a show to plan and perform before an audience that very afternoon.

Right away, Shirel noticed that the Arches were even more focused than the year before. "I saw how serious they are. They behaved differently from us," she said. "When they were [in Israel], they behaved like they were on a trip, a vacation." But, here, at home, "in the morning, we woke up at the time that Jessica told us. We were not used to this hour. Jessica tells you how to behave, and they did it! *Mishma'at!*" Discipline!

The Israelis and Americans showed each other what they'd learned in the last year so they could plan their first joint public performance. Dagan felt that his circus didn't have much to show.

Shai and Ali circled the ring on unicycles while clutching hands. Manar and Mysa demonstrated poi. Shirel, Manar, and Dana tried trapeze. Tamer and Ali showed how close they were to getting back handsprings.

Roey spied Iking, who was working in the circus's snack bar. Finally, he could share his news. "I know three diabolos!" he blurted out to his old friend.

Yes, in the weeks between the Galilee Circus's final show and their departure for America, Roey had mastered the trick. "It was a long process," he said. "It just got better and better every day. When I managed to hold on for about a minute, I started learning tricks.... Iking was shocked. He told me to go to the ring and show him right now."

Roey demonstrates three diabolos

99

"This Is What You Can Be"

Then it was the Arches' turn to show off. Balancing on globes, Alex and Shaina twirled hula hoops and Kellin juggled clubs and an apple, which he munched between tosses. Alex lay in the center of the ring while three Arches cartwheeled over her. Then they picked her up and flung her into the arms of two other troupers.

On their home turf, the Arches were even more impressive. In comparison, the Galilee kids' tricks seemed listless and static. "We found out we weren't that good," Shai said. "We weren't that good at all. We found out we can be much better. It was like putting a mirror right in front of us and telling us, 'This is what you can be. Work towards it.'"

Alex agreed that the Israelis had a lot of work to do, though she was impressed by their juggling. "Their acrobatic skills were very low," she said, "and they didn't have any aerial experience." Those areas—acrobatics and aerials—were the core of the Arches' strengths. How could the two groups possibly work together?

"We Didn't Have a Reason to Trust Them"

Jessica directed the American girls to develop acrobatics routines with the Israeli boys. "Elliana and I didn't want to be working with them," Alex said. "We did not want to get dropped. We trusted our guys. We didn't have a reason to trust [the Israelis]."

For their own protection, Alex and Elliana had to take responsibility; they had to make sure that their partners understood the safety guidelines. "We taught them the basics about being safe and being aware and learning each other in a way that won't hurt anyone," Alex said. "You always have to be aware of the other person's body as well as your own."

She knew these principles well, but she couldn't put them into words. Alex hadn't traveled to Israel the previous summer, and she was baffled by the language barrier. In fact, she was surprised to hear the Israelis speaking Hebrew.

Alex sits on Tamer Sanallah's shoulders

"I did not realize that Hebrew was a common language," she said. "I thought it was a religious language. So when they were speaking Hebrew, I did not understand why they were speaking their religious language."

Alex had to figure out how to use gestures and body language, as the others had already learned to do. "We did a lot of touching each other and grabbing each other's limbs and moving them around."

Despite her best efforts, both Ali and Tamer dropped her several times. To Alex, the guys seemed indifferent. "It didn't seem like a big deal to them," she said.

Fortunately, she was accustomed to being dropped and she wasn't hurt. "That's what happens when you work with new people," she said. "That's a normal part of circus."

Keaton, Manar, and Shai plan a show

In Israel, Jessica and Gilad had organized the acts. This year, the troupers had to do it themselves. Keaton took notes as they sat down and cobbled together their own series of tricks. "The kids tried to combine the moves," Ali said. "We said something. They [the coaches] said something—until we decided."

Ready or not—and they were not—the two troupes performed to a full house at City Museum on their second night together. The show concluded in an unsteady Galilee Arches Pyramid, with Shaina front and center, doing the splits.

Marc acknowledged that the Arches' presentation was "breathtaking" and that the Galilee Circus "came off okay." Dagan realized that some of his troupers were very embarrassed by their performance.

Manar felt insecure because she didn't have a special skill. She confided her concern to Shai, who pointed out that they were in a globe act together. "Yeah," Manar responded, "but I don't do anything in the globe act. I just stand there."

Nevertheless, the Galilee kids put into practice what they had learned during the past year—to smile and style through false starts, dropped balls, and wobbly landings.

Galilee Arches Day

The following day, the Galilee Arches performed for Mayor Francis Slay in an ornate reception room at City Hall in downtown St. Louis. This was their first daytime excursion, and Manar was surprised that the city wasn't as sprawling and gritty as she'd expected. "It doesn't look like I imagined," she exclaimed. "It's more beautiful."

Roey had a different reaction. "The first thing I realized," he said, "is that everything in America is bigger than in Israel—the stores, the cities, pretty much everything."

Since the troupers could hardly rig aerial equipment to the mayor's ceiling, the show highlighted acrobatics and tumbling, at which the Americans excelled, and juggling, at which the Israelis excelled. Still, it seemed to the Galileans that the kids who soared drew more gasps and applause from city officials than the jugglers.

The mayor declared August 1, 2008, "Galilee Arches Day." On behalf of the group, Shai and Lemond accepted the framed proclamation. Then, barefoot and sweaty, the Arches had their picture taken with the mayor.

By the fourth day, the Galileans had rehearsed more intensively than they usually did in several weeks back home. They had also performed more than they ordinarily did in an entire year—two daily shows at City Museum and one evening program in a park.

Mayor Francis Slay declares Galilee Arches Day

"We Stick Forever"

Shaina had to return to Illinois with her mother shortly after the Israelis arrived, so her friends celebrated her birthday two months early. This time the Arabs and Jews—and everyone else—hung out together.

The kids had downtime in St. Louis, just as they had in Israel. They dunked their toes in the Mississippi River and peered through windows at the top of the St. Louis Arch. They swam, fished, and shot bows and arrows in the Ozark Mountains. After Marc explained the rules of baseball, they attended a St. Louis

Cardinals–Los Angeles Dodgers game where the announcer introduced them over the loudspeaker.

One evening, Manar stepped outside and the City Museum door closed behind her. She was locked out. Fortunately, a kind couple saw her trying frantically to get back in. Manar was able to show them Circus Harmony's website on a cell phone, and they called Jessica, who came and let Manar back in.

Various kids were interviewed for newspapers, magazines, blogs, and radio and television programs. In an interview, Manar said about the Arabs and Jews in her circus, "We are friends. We stick forever."

The Israelis stayed in American homes one weekend. Roey and Yaron, along with Keaton, stayed with Elena Greene, a younger Circus Harmony trouper. Shai bunked with Max Pepose, whose home boasted a swimming pool, a gym, and a movie room.

In general, the Israeli kids politely ate the donated food that Jessica had arranged, though Shai complained that much of it was too oily and sugary. Thankfully, Whole Foods delivered hummus and pita on a regular basis.

Midway through their American adventure, Jessica woke up the troupers even earlier than usual for a bus excursion to Chicago. They had been given tickets to see Cirque du Soleil's one-hundredth performance of *Kooza*. Shai was so inspired that he bought a bracelet emblazoned with the line, "When I grow up, I'm going to run away to the circus."

Afterward, the Galilee Arches talked with performers and discovered that the contortionists were their own age. The Cirque teens were homeschooled, like Kellin, Keaton, and Elliana—except not actually at home and not by their mothers. They only saw their families during vacations.

The next day, the Galilee Circus kids were strapped into safety harnesses and given lessons in trick horseback riding. As Orly filmed her son, Roey lost his balance. The harness swung him up in the air and the horse cantered on without him. Unable to

Manar and Elliana are interviewed on the radio

Manar learns voltige

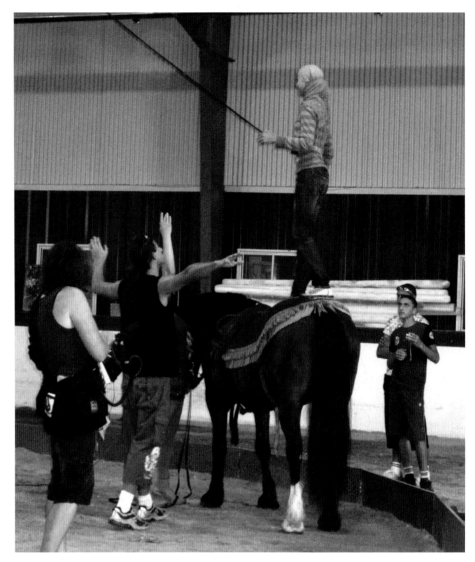

control the movement of the harness, Roey slammed into Dagan, who was standing in the middle of the ring. Dagan flipped over backward and both of them fell to the ground, the breath knocked out of them. Watching from the bleachers, Keaton shouted, "Ride like a maniac!" Fortunately, Roey and Dagan were okay.

Alex, Dana Raz, and Claire triple team on the trapeze

"Not Beyond Our Reach"

Having seen what kids their age could accomplish, the Israelis focused on improving their skills and on melding their acts with those of the Arches. Matt winced watching Manar wobble on Claire's shoulders. When they couldn't explain in English what they wanted to do, they continued to demonstrate.

The groups discovered that both did the same unicycle routine—pedaling around each other while holding hands—but called it different names. The Israelis called the trick *Sovivich*—Spinning. The Arches called it Pinwheel. Together, they embellished the act so that four Arches rode on their unicycles in the middle of the

Sariya Saabye was a world-class, Elite-level power tumbler. "It's rigid and it's structured," she said about the sport. However, "In circus, you can…take those tricks and say, 'Let's get into it or out of it in a different way. Or, let's add a person here. Let's jazz it up and do something different.' The circus gave me that freedom to take…skills without a lot of flair and make [them] a lot more showy and fun."

ring while four Israelis *soviviched* around them. Then they further enhanced it by changing partners—"like when you're square dancing," Shai explained.

Sometimes, a common language came to the rescue. Shai could plan a rolla-bolla act in English with Keaton and then explain it to Noam and Ahmed in Hebrew.

After a week or so together, the Galilee Arches began staging more complex performances. Kellin tried out flower sticks. Manal and Ahmed passed juggling rings, and Kellin and Yaron passed clubs. Roey juggled three diabolos, still a trick that only he could do. He was so nervous in front of an audience that his hands got sweaty and slippery, but he managed to keep going.

Alex triple-teamed with Claire and Dana on a single trapeze, flanked by Elliana and Shirel, each on her own trapeze. Choreographing the act, Alex made a discovery. "None of them speak perfect, fluent English," she said, "but it's not like they even need to. Somehow, we just understand each other."

Of course, they closed each performance with a Galilee Arches Pyramid.

After their final show, Sariya conducted an acrobatics clinic with the Israelis, focusing on basic skills. She noticed that a couple of the boys "had a natural affinity for basing."

She couldn't try anything too complex or daring, though. "The girls were weak," she said, "really weak. You can't do much with them. It's dangerous."

She also needed to develop different exercises for Manar, whose body-covering clothing could pose a risk. "I don't let my kids in acrobatics wear anything loose fitting or wear pants or sleeves because you have to grab each other…. Safety is the very first thing," Sariya said. "We had to work around that… Death Drop was one we couldn't do with her because you have to hold ankles, and she had [clothing] over her ankles."

But working around performers' weaknesses, fears, and religious practices is part of what makes circus appealing. "Not

everybody fits the same mold," Sariya explained. "That keeps it interesting."

With constant practice and Sariya's discreet guidance, Tamer and Ali pulled off back handsprings for the very first time, just before the circuses split apart. Everyone was surprised because they'd been practicing in secret.

The Galilee kids noticed the differences in coaching styles between Sariya, who adapted to their abilities and needs, and Dagan, who got impatient and yelled. Having now observed proper coaching, Marc said, "It was amazing what it was possible to learn in such a short time. It showed us that the Arches' impressive feats of acrobatic showmanship are not beyond our reach with proper coaching, a little courage, and calluses."

Jessica pointed out, "When you concentrate on what you can do together and on your similarities rather than what your differences are, you can create something amazing."

"I Want to Bungee!"

The Israelis agreed with Jessica in principle, but they knew that they hadn't yet created anything amazing. On everyone's mind was the question of whether they'd ever be able to do anything together again. This Go in peace/*Ma'assalama*/*Tzehu le Shalom* might be their last.

Even if that was the case, though, they'd gotten inspired. "We have to be better!" Roey insisted. "We have to practice more."

Marc thought his troupe was ready for the challenge. "We came away, all of us," he commented, "with a new appreciation of the difference between an after-school club and a real circus. We saw what is involved in making the transition—hard work, commitment, constant performance before an audience, showmanship (not just skills). And all of us came home ready to step up to the next level."

As a former circus student and performer himself, Dagan knew what it would take to move the Galilee Circus closer to the

Arches' level. So on the trip home, he challenged them. "Okay, you want to be like the Arches?" he asked. "Let's go.... You have to be ready to work a lot and make a lot of effort."

The moment Roey saw his dad, he blurted out, "I want to bungee!" For a child with phobias, this was a major announcement. His parents knew that he was really saying, "Now I can do everything." They were thrilled at how the circus had transformed their son.

Before the Israelis left for St. Louis, Ahmed had been coached to memorize one-word responses to simple questions. Now he was returning home with confidence and, for the first time, friends. His parents thought the circus and the trip had performed magic.

The pride and determination that Roey and Ahmed were developing were traits that all of the Galilee kids could acquire, if they were willing to make the commitment. But once again, schedules got in the way.

Ramadan consumed the month of September. And as soon as it ended, the Jewish holidays started. The members of the Galilee Circus would have to wait until the third week of October—nine weeks after their return from St. Louis—to resume regular practice.

CHAPTER EIGHT

BACK HOME: THE GALILEE CIRCUS 2008–2010

When the Galilee Circus troupers finally regrouped near the end of October 2008, they greeted each other excitedly. Except for the Asadi family, most of the kids who had traveled to America had not seen one another for two months, but they felt even closer now. "The trip definitely strengthened the bond," Roey said. Shai noticed that they also felt a closer connection to the big wide world of circus.

For those who had stayed home, the separation had lasted even longer. They had a lot to catch up on. And they all had a lot of work to do to catch up to the Arches, who hardly ever took a break. Muttering that the Arches didn't have to set up and put away their circus twice a week, they dragged mats, globes, balls, trapeze, diabolos, and rolla bollas from the storage closet.

Dagan gathered everyone together. He had lots of news and plans to share. He told the kids that he planned to divide the troupers into beginner and upper-level groups which would practice separately. By popular demand, the troupe would start working more on acrobatics. And the circus would meet twice a week for ninety minutes—double the previous amount of time.

For the kids like Roey, Shai, and Yaron, who wanted to perform at a more professional level or maybe even go pro, these plans sounded great. They knew that Sariya was right. "You've got

"If I don't respect [my teachers], I don't think I will be a success at circus."

—Hla Asadi

Roey's house in Karmiel

to be strong," she had said. "Tumbling or doing acrobatics for an hour a week is not going to get it done."

"I Do It Because the Teachers Want That"

Along with a group of other kids, Hla faced the wall, bent over, put her hands on the floor, and straightened her legs. Then she tried to swing her legs up against the wall. Propping herself up in a hand stand would increase her upper-body strength.

Although many of the kids had favorite—and least favorite—activities, Dagan wanted everyone to try a range of skills, including acrobatics, trapeze, and juggling.

Hla hated juggling. "It's boring to me," she said. Nevertheless, she agreed to give it a shot. "I do it because the teachers want that, and you have to respect them. If I don't respect them, I don't think I will be a success at circus." Her first love was still contortion. After several months of work and coaching from Leonid, she was able to lie on her stomach, curl her legs up and over her shoulders, and plant her feet beside her ears.

Hala also stretched herself into new shapes. She accomplished a sort of side-split, though she wasn't entirely satisfied. Her back knee was bent and her front leg was askew. "It was not beautiful," she confessed. There was still work to be done.

Roey concentrated on making his triple-diabolo tricks even trickier, but after a while juggling became tedious. He started to focus more on tumbling and acrobatics. Through dogged determination and will, he finally pulled off a round-off back tuck. But it scared him so much that he didn't try it again.

"It's Not Really Acceptable for Girls to Go Practice with Boys"

Before their association with the Arches, the Galilee Circus had done very little tumbling or acrobatics, and certainly not partner acrobatics. In fact, many of their partner acts involved jugglers, who generally stood at a distance from one another.

The Galileans practice hand stands

The Galileans practice a pyramid

The Arches stood on shoulders and held each other by the hand, the hip, the thigh, or the buttocks. They put their heads between each other's legs. The Americans were long accustomed to this physical intimacy, both between boys and girls and between members of the same sex. If the Galileans were going to emulate the Arches, they would have to touch each other in the same ways.

The Jewish Israelis quickly learned to take it in stride. The girls were more daring than the Arabs. They wore short skirts and tank tops on the street and bikinis at the beach. They sometimes complained that Arab boys heckled them because of their revealing clothing.

111

The Arabs, especially the girls—and most especially, Manar and Hla—were more modest. Now everyone in the troupe, regardless of cultural expectations or prohibitions, was being coached to handle each other—literally. The Arab boys and girls were embarrassed.

"In our society," Hala said, "we're a little bit conservative. It's not really acceptable for girls to go practice with boys, especially when our body is the thing that we work on." Although Manar and Hla were fully covered, their shiny leotards were skin-tight, revealing every curve. Manal and Hala wore short skirts and scoop-necked tops.

Manar, Manal, Hala, and Hla lived in the same house as their fathers' parents. Their grandfather was the head of their school and familiar with the ways of teenagers. He did not object to the girls' outfits. Their grandmother, however, disapproved. Although Hla loved and respected her grandmother, she dismissed the older woman's thinking, calling it "primitive."

After several months, the Arab troupers realized that touching was "part of the game" in circus. Hla said, "My family don't care because they know [boys] are touching me just because we're practicing together. We're friends, just friends.... They know they're not touching me for another reason." In fact, when they got new body-hugging costumes, she said, "New clothes for the show—that's cool!"

"We're Splitting into Groups"

Through longer and more disciplined practice sessions, the Galilee Circus began to strengthen, tone, and mold their bodies. A few tricks that had originated in St. Louis started showing up in northern Israel.

Before a performance, they gathered in a circle, stacked and raised their hands, and shouted *"Kirkas Galil!"* And they capped every show with a Pyramid. The Galileans' stance remained less

Hla and Ali Hasarme practice a Two-High

sturdy and their holds less secure than the Arches,' but the more they worked, the stronger they became.

Manar continued to fret about what she'd told Shai in America: "I don't do anything." While many of the kids relished the extra time they were spending at circus and the skills they were developing, Manar was feeling out of place. She showed up for practice less and less often and, by the end of 2008, she stopped going to circus altogether.

Shai felt that Manar "was a friend with everyone at the circus.… [She] was the glue binding us together. When she quit," he said, "I started noticing we're splitting into groups." Rather than being a friendly whole, they peeled off by skill areas. The jugglers congregated separately from the aerialists, and the younger Arab boys, especially those who liked to tumble, hung around Ali.

Shai still chafed under Dagan's coaching and leadership style. "We didn't really know Dagan well," he said, "and Dagan wasn't really experienced at being a head of the circus.… [He] used to yell at the circus whenever we didn't do something he wanted us to do. And sometimes he would say insulting words." When performers didn't perform well, he'd call them stupid.

Shai complained to other kids and talked back to Dagan. Finally, another staff member accused Shai of causing "an open rebellion" against Dagan.

Shai was already feeling on the fringe. Kids made fun of him. Manar left. Noam refused to do their staff routine. Roey preferred to juggle with Yaron. So Shai quit circus too.

His absence, however, was brief—so brief that some kids weren't even aware that he'd dropped out. After a couple of weeks, he realized he wanted to return. Shai liked being a "circus freak," as kids at school called him. Over the next two years, his skills grew. He learned to do front handsprings. He could juggle five balls. He developed a unicycle routine and also a partner rolla-bolla act. Many Jewish and Arab high schools require students to volunteer at a community project. Shai came to circus an extra day each week to teach juggling to the younger kids.

Except for Shai, the kids got along—inside the gym. The precept in circus was "everyone accepts you the way you are." As soon as the troupers walked outside the gym's doors, though, they entered another world entirely.

"We Don't Have Anything Against Anyone"

In early November 2008, posters popped up on lampposts around Roey's hometown. They stated, "My House Is Not for Sale."

This declaration was not directed at real estate agents. It was a campaign slogan from a new political party called My House. The party's candidates, who were running for election to the Karmiel City Council, believed that the town should remain Jewish—all Jewish. No Arabs allowed.

Zoning laws regulated the expansion of towns into the Galilee's green space. The Jewish town continued to sprawl as its population grew, while the Arab village was restricted to its current boundaries. The only places for them to build more housing were either closer to their neighbors or on top of their relatives.

Some Arab villagers had been moving to Karmiel for this reason; there was no more room in their towns. Now about 10 percent of Karmiel's population was Arab. Hla's mother, Sameha, who yearned for privacy, space, and quiet, wished she could join them.

Members and supporters of My House wanted other Arabs to stop moving there, and they wanted Jews to stop selling them their homes. Oren Milstein, the party's founder, stated, "We don't have anything against anyone. We are just in favor of our [Jewish] character."

Fourteen miles away, in the ancient city of Akko, Jews and Arabs lived side by side. Generally, they did so peacefully. But a month before the election in Karmiel, there were clashes in Akko on Yom Kippur, which is normally a holy and quiet day.

The My House candidates pointed to the violence in Akko, implying that it could also happen in Karmiel if Arabs kept moving in. Many Jews equated "Arab" with "terrorist." Other Jews chimed in, saying that they didn't want a mosque in their town, with a muezzin calling Muslims to prayer through a loudspeaker five times a day. A member of the City Council said, "Just as Arab boys marry Arab girls, we want our boys to marry our girls."

In the fall of 2008, Roey started attending a new school. The father of one of his classmates was involved in politics, and the elections were a topic of conversation in their classroom.

Roey knew, of course, that some Jews were anti-Arab. Noam and Yaron's father claimed that Israel was too small to contain both groups. He wanted all Arabs to be "transferred" to another country, any country. As far as Roey knew, Yaron did not agree with his father. But he was dismayed when he discovered that almost everyone at his school supported the position of the My House political party.

"Most of the kids," Roey said, "are really against the whole Arab-Jewish idea of being together…. They say racist comments… [such as] 'Arabs…shouldn't be here.'" Statements like this made him feel bad.

Initially, Roey tried to convince his friends that they were wrong. He discovered, though, that none of them listened to him. Hardly anyone at school knew that he participated in an Arab-Jewish circus, and he wasn't about to tell them.

In mid-November, the My House slate won three of the seventeen seats on the Karmiel City Council, and Milstein was chosen Deputy Mayor. An opposition party, called Karmiel for All of Us, proposed a mixed slate of both Arab and Jewish candidates. It didn't win any seats.

"In the Shade of a Patriot Antimissile Missile Launcher"

In the spring of 2009, Marc received an invitation that surprised him. The Israel Defense Forces wanted to know if the Galilee Circus would perform at a nearby air force base on *Yom Ha'atzmaut*—Israeli Independence Day.

Jewish Israelis observe *Yom Ha'atzmaut* much as Americans celebrate Independence Day, with outdoor concerts and firework displays. They also tour local military bases.

The next day, Israeli Arabs observe the *Nakba*—the anniversary of the Arab displacement following the founding of the modern state of Israel. Many visit the sites of Arab villages that the IDF destroyed in 1948 and hold demonstrations or strikes.

Marc worried that the Arab families might be upset if their children performed with Jewish kids on Israeli Independence Day—at a military installation, no less. So, he asked Ahmad for advice.

"Are there going to be planes?" Ahmad asked.

"Of course," Marc answered.

"So, what's the problem?"

Ahmad knew that the kids would love climbing inside the jets and watching flyovers at close range. Anyway, all of them were Israeli citizens. Even if, like most Arabs, they decided not to volunteer for the IDF when they graduated from high school, the base was as much theirs as it was the Jews'.

"So, there they were," Marc said, "Jews and Arabs, in the shade of a Patriot antimissile missile launcher, launching balls, rings, and each other into the air, to the enthusiastic applause of hundreds of [people] who had come out to show their children Israel's military might and eat ice cream."

The audience was so impressed that the following year, the troupe was invited back. As before, none of the Arab families objected to the circus's visiting an air force base. But Shai did.

"I decided that I'm a pacifist," he said. "I'm against wars and violence.... I will not take part in the division of the world population."

Shai considered boycotting the production, but he agreed to perform because of his love for the circus. He did not, however, tour the base or clamber into the planes. His decision led him to ponder whether or not to officially declare himself a pacifist. This path would have consequences two years later when, like almost all Jewish high school graduates, he would be drafted into the IDF.

Not long after their second visit to the base, the circus kids and their families took an excursion together to a beach near the Lebanon border. They hiked, shared food and recipes, chatted, and swam. The family members watched the kids perform. This joint outing became an annual circus tradition, each year in a different setting.

The Galilee Circus performs

Marc later wrote about these ordinary-seeming yet extraordinary outings: "The people so naturally chopping cucumbers and arguing about the number of falafel balls and chasing their kids around the picnic ground and joking with their peers were all Israelis, but comprised two populations.… [T]hey were all conscious of the fact that probably 99 percent of their families and friends and neighbors had never had such an experience."

"The Secret Is to Perform as Frequently as Possible"

Roey propped a large mattress on a diagonal against a chair. He was determined to get a back handspring. The mattress would keep him from landing on his head when he failed. He stared at it for half an hour, repeating over and over what Leonid had been telling him. "Just jump backward. Just jump backward."

He turned around, raised his arms, and sat back as if in a chair. Then he pushed off with his legs—and landed flat on his back. He tried again. And again. And again. Finally he did it! He tried again and did it a second time. But not a third. He'd lost it. From then on, Roey kept trying and trying and trying to snag another back handspring.

By the winter of 2010, the Galilee Circus kids had been working for two years on acrobatics, tumbling, juggling, trapeze, balance, and contortion. In addition, Marc had sought and received more invitations for them to perform. "The secret," Marc had learned from Jessica and the Arches, "is to perform as frequently as possible. You can't just practice, practice, practice."

As a result, the circus began performing for groups of visiting American Jews. More schools in the area learned about this coexistence project as the troupers put on performances in their gyms. These groups and others gave the Galilee Circus opportunities to go beyond practice and put on live shows.

When the troupers learned that the Arches would be returning to Israel in mid-July 2010, they knew they'd improved. But had they improved enough?

118

Partnering with the Galilee Circus had introduced the Midwest-erners to the Middle East. As a result of their interactions with foreigners, as well as the rich mixture of their own varied back-grounds, the Americans were increasingly comfortable with the international and multicultural aspects of circus.

Many Arches, like Kellin, had begun circus as small children. Others, like Shaina, were second generation. Those who had started young had grown up together. As a result, they barely noticed the racial and socioeconomic differences within their tight-knit group. "We started working as little kids," Meghan said. "Preconceived notions [such as racism] were eradicated from a young age." As for differences in families' incomes, she added, "they were noticed but not judged."

It wasn't just white kids who felt this way. When Shaina started circus, most of the troupers were black. She didn't feel dis-criminated against, even when the group became more integrated. Iking said, "There was no race issue at all within the Arches. We were tight as a group.... Me, being one of the poorer kids for sure, I never felt disrespected."

Issues of race and class were on many people's minds dur-ing the presidential election in the fall of 2008. St. Louis County was one of the few in Missouri that voted for then-Senator Barack

"When you have the basics down, you can do anything."

—Warren Bacon

Rigging at Circus Harmony

Obama, as did the City of St. Louis. Almost every other county, including the suburban ones where Alex and Meghan lived, opted for his opponent, Senator John McCain. Voters also amended the Missouri Constitution, making English the state's official language. The majority of the citizens would not tolerate two languages, whereas in Israel, both Arabic and Hebrew are officially recognized.

When Obama was declared the winner, Alex's father told her, "Never in a million years would our founding fathers have imagined a black man as president. Look how far we've come." Alex's partner Junior was black and her school was racially integrated because of an area-wide busing program, so she didn't think the election of a black man was a big deal. By now, however, she understood the economic differences between her and her circus friends and why some of them used to call her "the rich girl."

The ease that Circus Harmony's black, white, immigrant, wealthy, and poor students felt with each other allowed them, as Jessica said, to focus on their similarities. Their shared goal—to become stellar performers—brought them together day after day.

"It Was a Huge Struggle for Me"

After two years with Circus Harmony, Meghan knew she wanted to join the Arches. She had already met some of the basic requirements, like back handsprings, but she was having trouble with other skills. The problem was her body.

"I wanted to do tumbling," Meghan said, "but I was really, really, really tall and really lanky." The most successful gymnasts are compact, muscular, and less than five feet tall—the exact opposite of Meghan's ectomorphic body type. "It was a huge struggle for me but something I've always wanted to do," Meghan said. "[Body type] makes everything about circus more difficult…because of momentum. There's a lot more of you to whip around."

Meghan also didn't have the muscle mass of many of the other Arches. So to beef up her skills—and, if she could, her body—she ramped up circus from once a week to all day every Saturday and Sunday. She also gave up soccer and tennis.

Meghan and Mei Ling Robin perform contortion

Taking advantage of her body's affinity for long, graceful lines and of her own passion for stretching and flexing, Meghan also worked on contortion with Mei Ling. Their coach was Rosa Yagaantsetseg, an immigrant from Mongolia. She was trained and, in turn, taught in the Russian/Mongolian style.

This approach demands and develops precision. It's not enough simply to do a trick. The performer must make every movement exactly the right way. When doing the splits, for instance, it's

121

As a young woman in Mongolia, **Rosa Yagaantsetseg** performed partner acrobatics on a galloping yak and won medals in multiple international competitions. "My [Mongolian] students start very young—four, five," she said, "and work very hard.... Practice six, seven days a week. My students work almost eight hours every day."

essential to sink all the way to the floor and keep the toes pointed.

Even though Meghan was naturally flexible, Rosa was not impressed. "First year I see Meghan," Rosa said, "her back [was] very bad.... After work, very good back." With back bends, Rosa explained, "you have to work on each vertebra...so the whole back is bending."

Alex was familiar with this style of training from working with Sacha. "It's very effective and very difficult," she said. "You spend a lot of time on the little details. When you do a hand stand, you do not just get to hold it if you're up there and not falling. Rosa will knock you down if you're not doing it correctly, if your shoulders aren't tight enough—if your hands aren't in the right position, if your back is arched."

The girls appreciated Rosa's exacting expectations. They wanted to get things just right too, even if that meant repeating the same position over and over and over again.

Iking, on the other hand, had been more impatient. Before he left the circus, he'd wanted to learn flashy moves. He once asked Warren, "Why don't we practice the big tricks?" Warren answered, "When you have the basics down, you can do anything." Until then, it wasn't safe to try more advanced moves.

"I Had to Go Through the Painful Part"

Sometimes, even having solid basics can't keep a performer safe. While Meghan was waiting to enter the ring one day, she had an accident—or, rather, an accident happened to her. "I was just walking in line, and some girl decides to kick up to a hand stand. And here I am. *Boop.* [My nose] got broken." There wasn't much she could do except stop the bleeding and try to keep the swelling down.

Two years later, Max dropped her. "We were doing the Star Roll-Down for the first time," she said, "and Max didn't hold up my back. So, *boop.* He blamed it on gravity. He wasn't even sorry!" This time, her nose didn't break. "It just bled a whole bunch."

"In the circus, there are three ways to get hurt," Jessica says. "You can mess up and make a mistake personally, which would be your personal error, or you can get hurt because of your partner's error, or because of equipment error."

Meghan was hurt twice because of partner errors. Alex hurt herself twice. She broke her foot while tumbling and was out of commission for ten weeks. A year later, she displaced her kneecap when she landed wrong doing a spinning trick. She was in so much pain that Iking had to carry her out of the ring, and she had to undergo surgery to repair the damage.

Hala fell off the tightwire and landed smack on her stomach. Shai landed on his nose doing a front flip from the mini-tramp while he was trying to convince a girl not to be afraid of it. Hla's neck hurt for a month after she fell from a trapeze just minutes before a show.

Kellin even claims that pain is one of his favorite parts of juggling. "All the broken nails, jammed fingers, calluses, getting hit in the head a lot really adds up. It's absolutely horrible. But, after you finally get the trick, it's really great."

Aerials can be particularly hurtful, especially Spanish web, because there's no way to take a break. "Whereas trapeze, you can sit on it," Elliana said, "a web you're always standing or holding on or holding your weight up in some way.…"

Why didn't she quit?

"My mom was like, 'If you want to do this, this is the price you have to pay.' That was always something that I was aware of—to be good at something I had to go through the painful part. There were times when I would cry, and I didn't want to do it. She was always like, 'You decided you want to do this, you have to see it through.' It was an incredible life lesson." Elliana also learned that, "You just kind of forget about the pain eventually."

Pain can be such a constant presence in their lives that the Arches have scrawled messages to each other on the chalkboard near the entrance to the ring:

Injury Rates In Youth Circus

It's hard to compare injury rates between circus and other physical activities. One study counted the total number of hours that children spent in particular athletic activities over a two-year period, and the number of times an accident occurred during those hours. The results indicated that, overall, an average of 127,500 hours passed between injuries in circus. The comparable rate for gymnastics was 7,000 hours between injuries. For cheerleading, it was only 500 hours.

Warren Bacon discovered his love of flying while in graduate school at Florida State University. Better at circus than as a research scientist, he partnered with Jessica on aerials and performed voltige and tumbling with various troupes. He was also shot out of a cannon for several years. Warren especially loves coaching. "I'm just a redneck cowboy who ran away from graduate school with a master's degree in molecular biology to join the circus and made a living wearing a leotard and tights," he said.

Pain is the price of wisdom.
Pain is just momentary lapses of judgment.
Pain hurts.

"If the Proper Technique Is Not There, There's No Safety"

How do performers prevent or at least reduce the chances of injury? One way is by working carefully and methodically with exemplary coaches.

"I teach very rigid progressions," Warren explained. "Each skill builds on something. If the proper technique is not there, there's no safety." For instance, when a tumbler does a forward roll, he has to tuck his chin; if he doesn't, he might mash his nose.

Elliana advises circus novices, "When you run and jump, keep your tongue in your mouth. If you fall, you might bite it. You like your tongue, don't you?"

Circus performers of all ages rely on professional riggers to attach their equipment securely and test it regularly. Also, troupers look out for each other. They sometimes serve as each other's spotters. Standing near a flyer or wire walker, Arches look like they're posing with their hands clasped smartly behind their backs. But they're always ready to reach out and protect the performer's head and neck if she stumbles or drops.

"Welcome to the St. Louis Arches!"

The 2008 annual show was called *Café Appassionato,* meaning "with passion." Like several other intermediate-level students, Meghan hoped that a good performance in the show would be her ticket to Archdom. She and Mei Ling performed a partner act as waitresses who were "Bending Over Backwards to Serve You." First Meghan curled into a back bend. Then Mei Ling wrapped her arms around Meghan's waist and flipped her own legs up in the air. She held on as Meghan slowly rose to standing.

After the show, Meghan said, "Jessica called us all out to do another final bow. She gave us a blue certificate and handed us clown noses, and we put them on each other. She took the micro-

Rosa spots Meghan as she performs the Marinelli Bend

phone and said, 'Welcome to the St. Louis Arches!'" Meghan was so excited that she called her father, who was working in the Middle East, where it was very early in the morning.

As an Arch, Meghan got to perform in Ringling's preshow. She also attended master classes taught by performers from other circuses that stopped in St. Louis. She and Rosa were especially pleased when several of Rosa's former students from Mongolia, now contortionists with Cirque Dreams, helped Meghan with a very challenging trick. Called Marinelli Bend, it was nicknamed the "iron jaw."

Standing before a low table, Meghan leaned forward and clamped her teeth around a mouth grip that was fixed to the top of a short pole bolted to a table. Then she lifted her feet off the ground, transferring her entire body weight to her jaws. She steadily raised her legs behind, above, and past her head, until the back of her waist nearly touched the top of her head, and her feet pointed toward the floor in front of her.

Yet Meghan still felt inferior to Rosa's Mongolian students. "They could do so much that I couldn't do," Meghan said. "The question is, how close is your head to your butt? How high is that leg when you're standing in that position? It's that extra oomph."

Rosa was very proud of her American student, and she and Meghan developed a close relationship. "She took me in," Meghan said tearfully. "I was never a good tumbler. I wasn't very good at the whole acrobatic thing. I was not your typical Arch.... She stood up for me and my work."

"I Missed Circus a Lot"

Shaina did not return to St. Louis for almost a year after her early birthday celebration with the Galilee Circus in 2008. To keep up her circus skills, she did "the next best thing." She continued running track, which kept her in condition. And she kept driving the crowd wild at her school's sporting events.

"In cheerleading, you have to lift the girls, and you tumble," Shaina said. "So I just kept up with cheerleading."

There were a couple of big differences between the two activities. "With cheerleading, you're doing games like basketball and football games. And then there's a long period where you're not doing it. For circus, you do it year-round, and...people are cheering for you. I just like performing for people and making people happy." She also missed being cheered for. "I missed circus a lot," she admitted.

When Shaina came back to St. Louis in the summer of 2009, Jessica asked her to tumble out again with the Arches for the opening and closing sequences at Circus Flora. Shaina would have liked to participate in the acts too, but she couldn't because she hadn't been in town to practice.

That summer she spent all day, five or six days a week, at

circus. She discovered that, since several of the stronger Arches had moved on to higher-level circus programs, the remaining troupers had to build up their muscles. "We had to do a lot of conditioning to get up to where we needed to be," Shaina said. "I didn't really like it."

She decided that in her spare time, she'd create something brand new, so she worked up a swiveling aerial ladder routine. "I tried to have an act that was not seen before in the show," she said.

Shaina seemed to be dancing in air. The act made it into the regular Circus Harmony shows. She also did partner acrobatics, with Lil Donald. "It was easy," she said, "because you could throw him anywhere!"

After Shaina returned to Rock Island in the fall, she was injured during cheerleading. "We were lifting this girl up," Shaina said. "We're holding one foot, and she's holding the other, like a Y. She lost her balance and was falling forward."

Shaina's circus training kicked in. She realized, "No one else was going to catch her." Afraid that the girl would hit her head on the pavement, Shaina reached out. "I went to catch her, and she landed on my knee. She dislocated my knee and tore my meniscus."

Shaina was a hero but out of commission for nine months. She needed crutches for the first six months. Then a huge brace, which prevented her from bending her knee, for another three months. Then physical therapy. During that whole time, she missed both cheerleading and circus; however, the girl she saved continues to thank her.

Fortunately, she could play violin while sitting down. She maintained her chair position in her school orchestra and competed in solo and duet competitions sponsored by the Illinois Music Educators Association.

Shaina's cheerleading squad, 2010–11
Shaina is top row, third from left

"You Throw the Clubs behind Your Back"

Kellin hit a juggling plateau in 2008–2009. Bored with the sport and not advancing, he decided to learn trapeze and other aerials for a change. He worked up a comedy act on the Spanish web

Descended from generations of famously daring trapeze artists and high-wire walkers, **Alex Wallenda** grew up in the circus. It's like "growing up in a huge playground," he said. "Practice is developed through playing—one day on the flying trapeze, another on the trampoline." By playing and practicing, he found his own specialties—the high wire and juggling. And through performing with Circus Flora, he found his wife, Claire—Elliana's lyra partner! In keeping with his family's tradition, Alex and Claire perform together.

and created a slapstick clown routine with Keaton and Elliana. But when it came time for *Café Appassionato,* he returned to juggling.

One day in the fall of 2009, he happened to be standing in the Circus Harmony ring next to Alex Wallenda while Alex was practicing an intriguing maneuver called Three-Club Back Crosses. "That's where you throw the clubs behind your back with both hands," Kellin said.

He asked Alex for some tips. Kellin liked both the trick and the challenge of learning it. "I spent the whole summer of 2009 doing it," he said.

When he thought he'd finally got the technique, Kellin tried to show his friends. But whenever he did, he'd drop a club. He was frustrated but he knew that "it's always been like that for every juggler." Just when jugglers think they've got a juggling pattern down, they find out that they don't.

The following year, Kellin incorporated both acrobatics and contortion into his acts for the annual show, called *Fermata,* meaning "a prolonged note." But there was one trick Kellin couldn't do anymore. He'd lost his ability to do back handsprings. This was different from Three-Club Back Crosses, which he could throw into an act when he felt like it—or not, if he didn't. Back handsprings were mandatory for Arches. Since he'd lost the trick, his mother kicked him out. Kellin was demoted from Arch to Intermediate.

For a while, Kellin didn't mind his new, lower status. In fact, he enjoyed it. "You didn't have to do any work," he said. Kellin continued to work on juggling but not much else, including school.

School was still a rather haphazard affair for him. That year Jessica signed him up for a homeschool program that met once a week in a Catholic church. Parents were supposed to supervise their children's work the rest of the time, but that didn't always happen. If Kellin didn't finish an assignment one week, he'd do it the next—maybe. In any given semester, he wasn't sure what he'd take the next. To earn credit for high school graduation, he took a test at the end of the school year. This informality suited Kellin.

"School's not something that goes through my mind," he said.

He missed the thrills of being an Arch, though. The only trick he was allowed to do at Circus Flora was walking on stilts.

Jessica recognized that there were problems with the Circus Harmony hierarchy. Many troupers aspired to be Arches, but then, like Iking, discovered her demands. "It's your whole life," Jessica explained. "You miss birthday parties. You can't be in competitive sports. You've got to fight me to go to prom sometimes."

Some young people saw the pressure and decided not to join the Arches. Elena was a dancer as well as a circus performer. "I definitely thought about getting to be part of that," she said, "but the Arches is so time-consuming, and it's a lot of dedication. Being an Arch, I'd have to give up too much of my dance training."

Some kids saw the intermediate level as punishment. Jessica wanted to find a graceful way to help students find their level, but she didn't know how. Meanwhile, Kellin tried to regain his back handspring and his status as an Arch.

"I Genuinely Didn't Know What to Do with Myself"

Alex felt stymied. Like Kellin, she preferred to specialize. Flying trapeze was her first love, but there was no way to rig one in Circus Harmony's small, low space. So she continued to do aerials on static trapeze and other apparatus.

She maintained most of the basic Arches requirements but her heart was not in tumbling or juggling. "I have very bad hand-eye coordination skills," Alex said. "Some people pick up juggling so easily. It's very difficult for me."

Her body was changing, which was also challenging. Sariya pointed out that many girls who are involved in acrobatics, tumbling, and gymnastics find that puberty affects their athletic abilities in ways they can't anticipate. "Things you could do before, now you can't do because you're proportioned differently," she explained.

Kellin juggles on the tightwire during Fermata

129

Most unsettling of all, Alex's long-time acrobatics partner Junior was accepted at *l'École nationale de cirque*. Everyone was tremendously excited for him, but when he left for this prestigious professional program in the fall of 2009, Alex lost her base, both physically and emotionally.

"Junior leaving changed my life," Alex acknowledged. "I genuinely didn't know what to do with myself. I was only twelve but had been—literally—working hand-in-hand with Junior for four years." They were such a close team that they didn't even have to plan or rehearse their acts before they performed them. "When we got into the ring, Junior would whisper in my ear what to do next, and I would listen."

Alex had to switch positions for many acts. "That was the first time I wasn't a flyer," she said. "I was a base. It was really hard because everything I had trained for was no longer applicable."

Junior's departure even affected her solo acts. She felt that her daring One-Knee Drops on the static trapeze depended on a spotter she could rely on 100 percent. Without Junior, she hesitated to perform the trick.

Alex had lost not just a circus partner but also a dear friend. "He was the person I trusted most in the world," she said. Tears poured down her flushed cheeks when she had to say goodbye to him.

"Being Graceful Is Really, Really Boring"

Alex became impatient with some of Jessica's restrictions—particularly the dress code. Circus Harmony's style was more traditional and conservative than some other social circuses. Jessica expected her performers to maintain decorum. And she did not tolerate what she considered adult subject matter—sex, swearing, drugs, or alcohol.

Jessica objected when Alex began to rehearse in low-cut tops that revealed her cleavage. She told Alex that her appearance would distract her partners as well as observers. Nevertheless, Alex continued to choose her own wardrobe, including thong-back leotards. Jessica made her wear shorts over those. For safety reasons Jessica also directed Alex to remove her nose ring. She did so— but then covered the hole with a brightly colored band-aid, which Jessica told her looked silly.

Alex began to feel uncertain about her place in circus. Sariya could tell that she wondered whether or not she even belonged. Fortunately, Meghan, Elliana, and the other girls understood because they had gone through similar changes. They assured her that the circus definitely needed her.

Instead of quitting, Alex found ways to make her acts stronger, more muscular. "My big thing is swinging and doing drops. I think being graceful is really, really boring," she said. Her trapeze routines in *Café Appassionato* were fast-paced, and her drops, with the rope wrapped around her ankle, were startlingly dramatic.

The following year, Alex upped the ante in *Fermata*. She did acrobatics in the cube (an open metal box suspended from the ceiling), contortion, a ladder routine with Iking, tumbling, and silks. "Silks," Alex exclaimed, "is painful, requires determination and strength, and, at times, it's really discouraging. But, at the same time, it is invigorating, addicting, and relieving!"

She even started to learn to do a Hair Hang that year, a feat that is just what it sounds like. Despite having developed a high tolerance for pain, Alex exclaimed, "It hurt like hell!" She decided not to perform the trick in *Fermata*, not only because of the pain but also because she worried that her hair would fall out. Unsure of her next niche, Alex threw herself, sometimes literally, into almost every demanding skill she could find.

"They Care So Much about Me"

"What is wrong with you?!" Donald yelled at Iking. "You're tremendously talented. You wasting it doing stupid things."

Except for a brief stint with Circus Flora, Iking had not practiced or performed with the circus since the Arches returned from Israel in July 2007. Athletics kept him busy at school in the fall. But

Alex and Iking perform a ladder act in Fermata

team sports and school ended for the summer, and he got into trouble again. This trouble, though, was bigger than the usual kind.

One night in spring 2009, Iking was driving a car that a friend told him his parents had just bought. Somehow, Iking drove the car into a wall. He and his friend were knocked unconscious. When the police arrived, Iking learned that the car had been stolen. "I didn't know it was stolen," Iking protested. "We had the key."

He spent the rest of the night in the hospital. When a policeman took him home the next morning, his grandmother screamed at him, driving him out of the house. He was sleeping at his friend's house when Donald and Diane arrived.

"They could have just let me go," Iking said. "But they care so much about me. I wasn't none of their student anymore. I was just a regular kid that came and left." Iking realized that they could easily have ignored or abandoned him. "But they heard about the situation and came...sat me down and talked to me."

His former coach and his former mentor got his attention. Iking knew that he could have ended up in jail, like one of his brothers, or debilitated, like another, or dead, like too many friends.

"I realized I was doing stupid things," he said. "I had a good thing going with the circus. I could have stuck around there. When I was in circus, I was not getting in any trouble. So I felt I'm just going to use my head from now on. I'm just gonna do the right thing. I'm gonna stick with circus 'cause it probably could help me out in the long run."

But before he returned to circus, Iking had more opportunities to get into trouble. In addition to skipping classes, he got into fights. The worst one took place during the spring of his junior year in high school, not long after the car accident. "They called it a gang fight," Iking admitted. "And the police come."

He was suspended from school for the entire last quarter of his junior year and was assigned to an alternative campus for troublemakers for the first semester of senior year. But first, he was sent to jail.

"At the Justice Center, sitting up for a day and a half, I was so bored," he said. "I was sitting in that little box. Oh, my gosh. This is not me. That made me realize that if I mess up again, I could end up here for the rest of my life."

That experience scared Iking into making sure that that was his final fight. He determined that he would do right and set goals, like graduating from high school and going to college. He struggled every day to put what he wanted to achieve in the front. "And I put the things I don't want in the back."

To meet his goals, he had to get back to circus.

"Always Have Circus in My Pocket"

For the first time in two years, Iking went to see his old Arches friends perform at Circus Flora. As the flyer on a Two-High, Alex lifted Kellin and another Arch for a rotating He-Man. At the finale, Shaina, who also had been absent from circus, tumbled out with her troupe.

Iking reads while riding a unicycle at a bookstore

Iking decided to return to circus but not yet to the Arches. Instead, he opted to take Level 2 classes over the summer and during the fall so that he could play basketball during his senior year in high school. "I could be in the circus without having a big commitment," he said. "My goal was to always have circus in my pocket so I can go back to it and go further when I wanted to.… I wasn't 100 percent dedicated to circus."

After basketball season ended, Iking returned to the Arches during his senior year of high school. He spent even more time at circus than the others. In addition to training, taking classes, and performing, he also taught beginner courses at City Museum and at after-school programs for low-income students.

"Those kind of kids remind me of myself," he said. Remembering how Donald, Diane, and circus saved him, he added, "I will be pushing them harder to be better."

Because he had missed the last quarter of his junior year, Iking had to go to summer school after the end of his senior year. In addition to writing a paper, he had to take PE. He managed to get his work done so that, to his great relief, he could graduate in 2010. This meant that he could go back to Israel with the Arches that summer—and then spend a year preparing for his audition at *l'École nationale de cirque.*

> *"You must hate the behavior, not the people."*
>
> —Hla Asadi

The Galilee Circus kids had their signs ready to welcome the Arches when they returned to Israel in the summer of 2010.

The Israeli Circus Welcomes You.
You Reached Your New Home.
Sababa!

But there had been a time-zone mix-up, and the Arches weren't actually scheduled to arrive until the next day. Instead of spending that evening getting reacquainted with their friends from America, the Galilee troupers stayed overnight at a nearby guesthouse by themselves.

The next day they trekked back to the airport in Tel Aviv with their welcome signs. The Galileans greeted everyone enthusiastically, even the Arches they had never met. Shirel was particularly excited to see Alex; they had kept in touch on Facebook over the past two years.

"It was weird because I didn't know anyone, and people are giving me hugs!" Meghan said. It was also the first visit to Israel for Alex, Melvin, and Lil Donald.

This time, most of the travelers were older and more self-sufficient than the 2007 group. But Lil Donald was only ten years old, venturing to a foreign country with only his circus family—

The Galileans welcome the Arches to Israel

no immediate family, not even Shaina—to support him if he got homesick. Having heard that he would be served salad for breakfast and hummus and mashed eggplant for lunch, he arrived lugging an entire suitcase stuffed with cereal bars and packets of Ramen noodles.

"We Are All As One." Or Are We?

"In the few weeks before they came," Roey said, "we really practiced a lot on the acts." Following the Arches' lead, the Galileans had also performed for a large number of audiences in the area.

Their efforts were beginning to pay off, as some of the Arches noticed when the two circuses started rehearsals. Even Kellin acknowledged that their juggling skills were close to top-notch.

Iking agreed. At their first joint practice session, he saw "a big improvement" since the last time he'd seen them. "Their diabolo level was through the roof!" he exclaimed. "They were amazing jugglers. Their presence in the ring was so much better. And the way they worked was totally different—they were being more attentive in practice.… It was much easier to create a show."

Troupers stack hands for "Ga-li-leeeee Aaaarrr-ches!"

Creating a show was easier because the Galilee Circus could do more tricks now. Shai realized that they could finally combine routines to do some partner acrobatics with the Arches. During rehearsals, Jessica couldn't always tell which trouper had been trained in which circus.

But some of the Americans concluded that the Israelis hadn't improved in all areas. Meghan observed that her troupe was "definitely more advanced" than the Galileans. Alex also felt that the Israelis' overall skills were still rudimentary compared to those the Americans displayed. "[They] required lots of training to learn the tricks that the Arches were working on," she said. "The girls had finally been more exposed to aerial work but they had little understanding of grace."

Still, the troupers were comfortable with one another now. "We work together," Dana said. "It doesn't matter with whom."

Hala added, "I was *sooo* happy. It was beautiful working with them!" Mysa agreed. "We are all as one," she said.

That wasn't true for everyone, however. On their fourth day together, Shai refused to get on the bus to a Druze village.

"Ali and two other Galilee Circus guys were throwing acorns at me," he said. Annoyed, Shai threw some back, and they hit a friend of Ali's. The two got into a wrestling match.

"I was about to hit him," Shai admitted, "when I noticed what I was doing.… I was a pacifist. I was about to betray my values. On top of that, I was about to hit someone from my circus. This is not the atmosphere that's supposed to be in a social Jewish-Arab circus."

Shai was miserable. This incident, combined with his feeling that the Galilee Circus was falling apart, convinced him to quit—again. But after Claire urged him to perform one more time with the group, he climbed on the bus and rejoined the tour.

"I Would Have Stayed Forever"

Alex found the trip to be a spiritual experience, especially her visit to the Church of the Holy Sepulcher. "I grew up with the basis of a Christian upbringing," she said, "however, it was never forced on either of us." Free of religious pressure but familiar with a Christian context, Alex was moved by the site of Jesus's crucifixion and burial. The Western Wall also affected her. "When I made a wish…I felt so blessed," she said.

Alex also loved the close family relationships in the Arab villages—"families on families on families," she said. The American visitors and their Jewish and Arab hosts were invited to a wedding in the Arab village, even though none of them knew either the bride or groom. She also became especially good friends with Roey and Shirel. "I would have stayed forever," she said.

Meghan didn't develop close personal relationships, but she enjoyed observing the architecture, the scenery, and the inter-actions. Iking found his second visit easier than his first. The last time hadn't quite seemed real. "I was so shocked," he said. But now he saw that "it wasn't a dream."

Iking performs in Tel Aviv

"Who Are We Performing for Here?"

When the Galilee Arches pulled into Levinsky Park on their last day together, they were expecting to perform for the children of immigrants. But when they got off the bus, they didn't see a single child. It turned out that the park had become a squatters' encampment—"home" for hundreds of otherwise homeless foreign workers in Israel, many of them from Sudan.

The situation didn't even look safe; the circus kids stood close together for protection. "Who are we performing for here?" someone asked.

In spite of their doubts, they pulled out their equipment and the mini-tramp. Pretty soon, a few children appeared, then

137

disappeared. After a while they reappeared with more children. More and more people flocked to the park, until the grounds were filled with youngsters and grown-ups. Other spectators stood on the roof of a nearby building.

Energized by the spontaneous crowd, the troupers threw themselves into their performance. The enthusiastic audience cheered the young acrobats, tumblers, and jugglers. Marc called it "the best show of the tour."

Afterward, a Sudanese-Israeli preteen walked up to the group and said in carefully composed English, "I want to learn." They had to explain that he couldn't join the circus because it wasn't based in Tel Aviv. As the two circuses split off once more, the Galileans vowed to keep learning, to keep striving for the Arches' level.

"Like Any Normal Place"

"The first time we saw each other after the Arches left was a great event," Shai said, laughing, "because we didn't have a home." Instead of getting together in their usual gym in Karmiel after the holidays in the fall of 2010, the members of the Galilee Circus converged on Ahmad's house.

During the previous year, the circus had started bumping into scheduling problems with the gym in Karmiel. The group wanted to hold longer and more frequent sessions, but the gym was booked.

Marc considered another facility; however, the area wasn't zoned appropriately. When he tried to convince the town to house the circus in one of its dozen or so other community centers, no one seemed interested in supporting the coexistence project. So, in its seventh year, the Jewish-Arab circus moved from Karmiel to Biane—from a Jewish town to an Arab village. The troupers felt welcome in Biane's spacious community center which was just minutes from Deir al-Asad. Several people worried whether Jews would be willing to travel to the Arab village. In the early years of the circus, one girl's father didn't want her to perform in a show there. Would he let her practice there twice a week, at night?

Furthermore, it was too expensive to continue to operate the bus that transported the kids from their villages to class. Marc decided to discontinue the service, hoping that the Jewish parents would drive their children to the new venue. Parents in farther-flung towns, such as Atzmon, complained loudly.

"I thought we're going to have less Jewish people in the circus and less Jewish people coming to shows because it's in an Arab village," Roey said. "Arab people don't mind walking into Jewish villages and into the mall…. It's a common thing. But no Jews are going into an Arab village."

As it turned out, he needn't have worried. None of the veterans balked. "We were so excited to see each other, and there were lots of hugging and lots of catching up," Shai said. "After that, we got all of our stuff from Ahmad's house to the new place."

But what about new Jewish students? Would they enroll? Some parents objected, but Dagan said, "They tried it a few times and found it's fine, like any normal place."

The proportions of troupers remained the same—almost but not quite an equal number of Arabs and Jews. Marc saw that as a sign of the circus's success. He did worry, though, that they might have lost some newcomers because of the lack of transportation.

The younger members continued to separate themselves, preferring to work with kids who spoke the same language, lived in the same village, and went to the same school. "You have to mix," Dagan told them. "You do it together."

And then there was an incident. A local Arab guy was buzzing by the gym on a loud motorcycle while Shai was trying to teach a class. "He was making noise…just to annoy us," Shai said. "It was really bothering the students." So Shai went outside and told him to stop. The next day, the motorcyclist brought friends, and they threw stones at Shai. One nearly hit his head.

Ahmad resolved the conflict by inviting everyone to a

Hla tries out the tightwire

meeting. "We made shalom," Ahmad said. For the time being, peace had been restored among the neighbors.

"We Got to an Understanding"

Around the same time, Oren Milstein was fired from his job as deputy mayor of Karmiel for discriminating against Arabs. Roey was glad to see him go. He did not, however, try to convince his friends and classmates of his view. He had come to the conclusion that such conversations were futile.

"I never talk religion and politics with friends because you never get to a good place," he said. "None of my friends have the same point of view that I do. They have a totally different point of view. They're not willing to hear anything else."

As a result, he still didn't even tell his school friends that he was in the circus, and certainly not that the circus met in Biane. "I know people," he added, "who think that if you go into an Arab village, you're going to get hurt; you're going to get lynched."

In fact, Roey had a frightening experience in a nearby Arab village where he, Yaron, and Ali went to perform at a party given by a friend of Ali's. Three local kids, suspecting that he was Jewish, surrounded him so that he couldn't get away. They asked him where he was from, why he was there, and who brought him. When he pointed to Ali, they backed off. Roey wondered if the local kids would have hurt him had he not come with an Arab friend.

He did not discuss the incident with either his schoolmates or his circus friends. The tradition at the circus remained, "When we get to the circus, we just do circus." Shai added, emphatically, "We. Do. Not. Talk. Politics."

One exception to that tradition arose on May 15, 2011. On that day—the *Nakba*—residents in Deir al-Asad went on strike and held a large protest rally.

"Everything in the whole village closed," Ahmad said. Parents of some Arab troupers asked him to close the circus as well. But for a change, he decided to bring the Jewish and Arab performers together for a discussion.

Ahmad asked them if they knew why the villagers were protesting. Roey explained what he knew about the history of the *Nakba*.

Ahmad asked, "What do you think about the Palestinians?"

Shai expressed sympathy for their situation. "It's a very sad day for them," he said.

Hala considered herself Palestinian as well as Israeli. "There was a little bit of tension because of the fact that the whole *Nakba* thing is between Arabs and Jews," she said. "We can talk together, and we're happy practicing together. But once the whole issue is brought up to a level where you bring up all of your stereotyped thinking, there can be a bit of a problem."

Unaccustomed to confronting the long-standing conflict openly, everyone felt awkward, tense, and somber. After quiet conversation, Hala said, "We got to an understanding." Yet, they hoped never to have to talk about these topics again.

Such stereotyped thinking did become a problem the following year. The circus was performing in Akko. Some Arab boys insulted Shirel, who was wearing her revealing circus costume on the street. "I hate this about Arabs." she said to Hla, "But I love you like a sister."

Hla was hurt and angered. She said to Shirel, "You must not think that all Arabs are like that. There are a lot of Jews who act the same way. You must hate the behavior, not the people. Don't say, 'I hate Arabs.' I hate Arabs who do that as well." Shirel agreed with her friend.

"Everybody in the Arches Knows Everything"

Meanwhile, the Galilee Circus expanded both its hours and its coaching staff. Hala, Hla, Roey, Shai, and the other members of the performing group started spending nine hours a week in the gym—seven in practice and two more teaching the beginners. Just three years ago, they had spent only an hour and a half per week in rehearsals.

Sarah Herr saw her first circus show when she was ten. She was so excited that she taught herself acrobatics, juggling, diabolo, and unicycle. She and a friend then performed duo acts with youth circuses in their native Germany. Since being trained as an instructor (in a program called *Zirkuspädagogik*), she's combined circus with dance, music, and drama, as well as safety. She spent a year teaching these skills at the Galilee Circus, as part of her college program. Sarah loves circus because it is "open to everybody who is interested, independently of the social or cultural background and independently of language."

This was great for circus but hard for academics. Roey was already spending over forty hours a week at high school, where he was majoring in physics and math. He also wanted to reserve time to compose songs on his guitar. Like some of the Arches, Roey had to figure out how to balance his personal priorities.

As a unit, the troupers also needed to set priorities for developing new skills. Sarah Herr, an aerialist from Germany, volunteered to coach and help the youth troupe rank its goals. She began by asking Dagan and the troupers a lot of questions. *What tricks do you want to learn this year? What methods have helped you learn them? What other methods do you need?* The answers helped the coaches plan practical steps for the performers to try to reach their goals.

Hala's goals included silks and acrobatics, as well as getting over her fear of the tightwire, which resulted from a fall four years earlier. Hla's goal: contortion. Roey's: diabolo, acrobatics, and tumbling, especially back handsprings and back tuck. Shai's: tumbling and juggling with new and different objects—hats.

Mostly, the Galilee Circus still wanted to do whatever the Arches did. Although several Israelis had begun to search circus websites and join online listservs, they had little experience with or exposure to other circuses and none to other youth circuses. For them, the Arches were the gold standard.

"Everybody in the Arches knows everything at a high level.… That's something we don't have," Roey said. He had noticed that, even though several ace Arches had graduated and left, the St. Louis circus was still doing many tricks that the Galileans still couldn't. "It was amazing," Roey added. "No matter who's in their circus, there's always someone in the same level." And that level was still higher than the level of the Galilee Circus.

"I Believe in Me"

Hala watched every move that Sarah made very closely. The new aerials coach was showing her how to climb silks. Because Sarah did not speak Arabic and her Hebrew was limited, she pointed to each body part and moved in slow motion.

Sarah wrapped her right leg around the fabric, first in front of it and then behind it, so that the silk crossed over the top of her foot. Then she flexed her foot. Step by small step, Hala made exactly the same moves. Then Sarah showed her where to place her hands on the fabric and pull herself up, how to place her left foot on top of her right and straighten her legs so that she slowly lifted herself off the mat and climbed up the silks.

Hala gave it a try. Pretty soon she was six feet in the air, then ten feet, then eighteen feet. She was scared to be up so high, but also exhilarated. She was relieved that Sarah stood right next to the silks, keeping her eyes on her as she climbed.

Hala had worked on the skills that everyone learned—some juggling, some acrobatics, some poi. When Sarah arrived, Hala watched her perform graceful and daring routines on the silks. Hala knew this was going to be her passion. With silks, she could combine acrobatics, contortion, and aerials.

Hala practices silks

When Hala had mastered those basic skills, Sarah added static positions, such as knee hooks and hangs. "Hala became very good in a short period of time," Sarah said. "She became very enthusiastic and ambitious. She trained a lot and kept practicing difficult things."

Eventually, Hala worked her way up to drops—free falls that are abruptly halted by a carefully tied knot. The first time she tried one, she cried out in fear. To gain the confidence to try bigger drops, Hala needed close guidance and "a little bit of pushing," Sarah said. "Silks can be very dangerous. They need full attention." It turned out that Hala was good at this too. "She was focused and very aware of even little movements, which is important while doing silks."

A young Jewish trouper named Einat Opalin helped coach Hala. Einat had studied silks for three years in Mexico before her family moved to Israel. She talked with Hala about finding her balance and about strength. "You have to support yourself, by yourself. It is a one-person job," Einat said.

Hala grew physically stronger doing silks and developed more body awareness. Within a year, the two girls created a partner act. Hala especially liked a routine called Vampire, in which they seemed to fly on black wings.

These successes with silks had another benefit for Hala. She grew more self-confident in other areas. Speaking about both Hala and Hla, Dagan said, "They were more secure in everything they did…because they succeeded. Also, they became…less afraid to try new things." Ever since Hala had fallen off the tightwire, she'd been afraid to get back up. Now more sure of herself, she decided to try it again. "I'm going to do it," she said to herself. "I've got confidence in myself. I believe in me."

"Hats Make Me Feel Special"

Shai had become entranced with a YouTube video of Lorenzo Mastropietro, an Italian juggler who manipulated hats. "I'd watch it over and over," Shai said.

Mastropietro's acts were funny as well as deft. He balanced a hat on his toe, flipped it in the air, spun around, and caught it on his toe again.

Shai wanted to do tricks like this, too, but he didn't have the right kind of hats—ones that were stiff and heavy. Then he happened across a circus shop in Barcelona during a family visit. The shop sold hats that were perfect for juggling. But his father refused to spend thirty euros (about forty dollars) per hat.

So Shai pulled out his juggling balls and went outside. "I made two euros in ten minutes," Shai said. "My dad told me, 'We have to go. I'll give you the money.'" Shai ordered three hats. Back in Israel, he began to experiment with this new medium.

Shai juggles hats

He faced several problems right from the start. The Galilee Circus no longer had a juggling coach, so Shai tried to teach himself through a mixture of online videos and trial and error. Also, his long hair got in the way. He had been growing it out for nearly three years to donate to children who had lost their own hair because of treatments for cancer.

Finally, in September 2011, Shai cut and donated his hair. He was ready to get serious about hat juggling. "I would get back from school and practice hard on hats," Shai said, "trying to create new tricks and trick combos." He imitated Mastropietro, whom Shai called "my inspiration for everything related to hats."

Individual tricks were fine but Shai needed a full act. Knowing that music could set the tone, he searched for a song. When he heard "Jolie Coquine" by the group Caravan Palace, he thought, *This could be my hat routine.* His guiding principle became matching the style and speed of his movements to the rhythm of the music.

"It was hard because it was very fast," Shai said. "This act had the most work put into it in the entire Galilee Circus history.... It was all I did for two weeks.... When I wasn't working on it, I was thinking about it."

Shai's mother worried that he spent more time juggling hats than he did on his homework. But because no one else at the Galilee Circus manipulated them, Shai realized, "hats make me feel special."

Unlike other members, he had not yet developed his own identity as a circus performer. Hla was the troupe's sole contortionist. Hala did silks. Roey outclassed everyone else with three diabolos. Now Shai was developing his unique expertise.

"We Are *Soooo* COOL!!!"

The members of the Galilee Circus made a video of themselves, which ended with the tagline, "We are not professionals...(yet)... but we are *soooo* COOL!!!" Just three years earlier, they had barely known these tricks existed and couldn't have imagined actually doing them.

In the spring of 2011, Sarah trained Hala, Shai, Roey, and other troupers in how to coach. This training consisted of ten classes in the fundamentals and safety rules for a range of skills— circus games, juggling, balance, acrobatics, aerials, dance, drama, and clowning. She also gave them guidelines for how to observe and communicate with students. The classes culminated in a three-day intensive workshop at a kibbutz, complete with a ninety-page manual, a written exam, and young students for them to train.

The performing group's schedule became especially hectic the following fall when another German coach volunteered to work with the Galilee Circus. Veronika Reichard, an actress and

veteran circus performer, proposed an idea for an entirely new kind of show.

Actually, it would be new for the Galilee Circus but it was somewhat similar to the annual shows that the Arches had been staging for years. The Galileans, however, had never seen or been involved in those shows, and they didn't have the equipment, space, costumes, funds, or music that the Arches did. Roey didn't think they could do it. But Shai, who volunteered to be the assistant director, had learned a lesson from Jessica: no matter what, never give up.

The Galilee Circus
Top row: Shai, Yahel Ritter, Einat Opalin, Shirel, Ali, Saeed Assaf, Roey, Yaron
On the floor: Hala, Ahmed Asadi, Samer Sanallah, Hla

CHAPTER ELEVEN

THE ST. LOUIS ARCHES 2010–2012

"Respect your discipline. Circus skills are just one part of it. You have to have respect for the show, respect for everything you do."

—Tom Dougherty

In the fall of both 2010 and 2011, the Arches performed for the Ringling preshow. They produced two annual shows—*Grazioso* ("graceful") in 2011 and *Tessitura* ("texture") in 2012. They also appeared with Circus Flora both years, as well as with Univer-SOUL Circus. All of this came on top of the classes, teaching, and shows that otherwise kept them tethered to the Circus Harmony ring in City Museum.

While maintaining this hectic schedule as a group, individual Arches underwent personal and professional revelations and transformations.

"You Don't Have to Style All the Time"

One weekend when Iking was staying at Jessica's house, he noticed that Kellin seemed absorbed in something on his computer. He asked Kellin what he was doing.

"Watching juggling videos," Kellin answered. "This is really cool juggling. I should start doing this." Kellin pointed to a juggler named Wes Peden.

"That's cool," Iking said. "I'm watching tumbling videos."

The guys looked at each other. Both of them, they realized, were seeking out and studying the best practitioners of their favorite circus art form. This was getting serious.

Unicycles hang from the ceiling at Circus Harmony

Kellin said, "We should get really good at what we're doing."

Kellin would soon turn fourteen. He'd finally regained his back handspring and his status as an Arch. But he'd been juggling for the Arches for almost eight years and felt both stalled at his level and bored with the sport. Now he was watching someone who was defining juggling in a completely different way. No rubber chickens. Hardly any recognizable individual tricks. Peden's style seemed to flow from one clever toss or manipulation to another, and Kellin found it intriguing.

"I realized I was really bad," Kellin said. "I was not even close to the level that I should be."

The new generation of jugglers was no longer working within the traditional "frame" in front of them. Beginners learn by tossing scarves or balls within the bounds of an imaginary rectangle, shoulder width and waist-to-forehead high. This simple geometry helps them keep their throws steady and even. Peden and others were experimenting with "body throws"—tricks that go all around the juggler's body.

Kellin performs at the IJA Juniors

Kellin had been throwing clubs under his leg or catching them behind his back for several years. But the new styles reached farther, both spatially and artistically.

Rather than remain stationary like most traditional jugglers, Peden seemed to dance around the floor as he threw three clubs ten or twelve feet in the air, caught one between two others in a scissors catch behind his knee, rolled them down his arm, tucked one under his chin, tipped them off of each other, and juggled them one-handed.

Kellin explored further. He found videos of Alexander Koblikov, a Ukrainian who could manage eleven balls. Gustaf Rosell could juggle entirely behind his back, with his eyes closed. Jay Gilligan tossed balls that were attached to strings and manipulated odd light fixtures on a darkened stage for visual effects.

Kellin's favorite juggler was Thom Wall, who was also from St. Louis. Wall pranced on the stage barefoot, incorporated sound

Richard Kennison taught himself to juggle when he was thirteen. The next day, he stood on his roof and taught nearly two dozen other kids. Over the last forty-five years—including almost twenty-five years coaching for Jessica—he's taught more than 200,000 people. Three of them have won the International Jugglers' Association Juniors competition. "I'm a teacher inside and out," Richard said. He even enjoys teaching beginners because of the *aha!* moment on their faces when they get it.

effects, held balls immobile on the bridge of his nose, clowned, and juggled seven balls with his hands and feet.

The common thread among these new, young jugglers was their fluid movement from one complex sequence into another and then another, rather than a succession of throw-and-catch flashes or stop-and-start tricks. Many of them refrained from whirling lots of objects into the air all the time. They paused. They even held onto a club or two, lengthening its dwell time, while they simply tossed the others up and down in their other hand. Their programs looked like ballet. Their style was called "art juggling."

"Art jugglers are like modern dance," Richard said. "It is a beautiful thing."

With help from Richard, Kellin set about finding his own personal style. He drew ideas not only from these breakout artists but also from old-time vaudeville. "I watched a lot of Bobby May videos," Kellin said, referring to a variety-show juggler popular in the 1920s and 1930s. May devised clever tricks in which he purposely dropped the club at a particular angle and rate so that it would bounce back up to him. He tossed a cigarette over his back and caught it in his lips. Then, he did the same with a lighted match, with which he lit the cigarette.

Performing frequently helped Kellin explore various styles of object manipulation. In *Tessitura*, he borrowed from both Rosell and Wall, juggling three balls behind his back with a fourth balanced on the bridge of his nose. From May, he learned a bounce-club technique and even figured out how to make clubs ricochet off each other.

The juggling personality that Kellin began to develop rejected one of the fundamental circus principles that his mother had taught him, the Arches, all of her other students, and the Galilee Circus. "You don't have to style all the time," he realized. "I stopped styling. I'm very proud of that decision.... All the big names in modern juggling were all doing fluid acts. They would pause for a little bit, to breathe, and the audience would naturally clap." Kellin sometimes signaled applause points by waggling his bushy eyebrows.

"I found what I wanted to do quickly compared to other jugglers," he said. "It took me about two years to get to a place where I juggled the way I felt fit me." He experimented with how long to hold a beat before moving on to another pattern, and how to keep the audience's attention. Most of his sequences were unique and didn't have names, other than ones he and Richard concocted, like "Scrambled Eggs" and "Kellin's Cool Move." They likened his approach to working with Legos—creating short building blocks of tricks, which he could compile and rearrange. He constructed routines by switching positions, alternating between slow and quick movements, and creating intriguing shapes with airborne props.

These progressions evolved very successfully. Between the summer of 2011 and the summer of 2012, Kellin won

- a "juggle-ship" (scholarship) to attend the International Juggling Association (IJA) in Rochester, Minnesota,

- his second Groundhog trophy—this one for being the "Most Marvelous" competitor at the Groundhog Day Jugglers Festival in Atlanta, Georgia,

- third place and $3,000 in St. Louis's Teen Talent Competition,

- the role of young King Arthur in Circus Flora's take on Camelot,

- and, most prestigious of all, $500 and the gold-medal Junior Championship Lucas Cup at the IJA in Winston-Salem, North Carolina.

"Kellin takes art juggling and traditional toss juggling and his own really wonderful subtle character. And, he blends it all together. It's really captivating," Richard said. "He's bridging the gap."

"I Changed the Way I Look at Life"

Iking definitely needed to "get really good" at what he was doing—preparing to audition for the highly respected and very competitive circus school, *l'École nationale de cirque* (ENC).

He also considered another school, *l'École de cirque de Québec*, but after looking into it more closely, he realized that it was not the best program for him. "The teachers are really good but the schedule is basically your own schedule. Do what you want to do," Iking said. "If I have a set schedule, I have to be there on time…. I need that push and that drive that forces me to work."

Simply applying to ENC was a daunting challenge. In fact, he had to apply to apply. First he had to submit written responses to such questions as "Describe in your own words what kind of circus artist you want to be." Iking's answer: "I want to be an *artiste* who can be used in a show in so many ways." He understood that versatile performers who have a wide range of skills are the most likely to get jobs. Only after his written questionnaire was accepted would he be able to go to Montreal to audition.

The audition would consist of three stages—Physical, Artistic, and Comprehensive. To be admitted, he'd have to pass each stage. The Physical tests progress from front rolls to back handsprings, from leg lifts to squat jumps, from back bends to splits. He'd have to demonstrate his flexibility and present a routine, as well as act, dance, and improvise.

During the summer after he graduated from high school, Iking taught classes at Circus Harmony during the day, five days a week, and worked out every night at gymnastics gyms around town. He knew that he needed to prepare bigger tricks than he'd been able to, tricks that required foam pits and large trampolines. He compiled a list of the acrobatics and tumbling goals he wanted to accomplish before he applied to the school:

Standing whip, full in tuck out
Round-off double full, double back
Kick full—double and triple

Iking, wearing a
Circus Harmony T-shirt

152

Back headspring
Back tuck to back
Standing back full punch front one-half
Triple back (solid)
Front one and three-quarters into crazy combo
Solid double—layout and pike
Full in, full out
Double full in—back out or full out
Double side back
Sitting full twist

He had less than three months to learn all of these tricks. "I never worked so hard for something in my life," Iking said.

For acting classes, he turned to Tom Dougherty, a former clown coach. Iking knew that clowns provide much more than funny gaffes in the ring. Through a subtle shrug or drooping head, they silently tell a tale and convey a range of emotions that entrances the audience as effectively as actors on a stage.

On some days, Tom gave Iking surprising assignments. Iking would come to circus expecting to practice pikes for his audition, but Tom would make him sweep the bleachers or paint the pillars instead.

"How's that going to help me?" Iking asked him.

"It's going to help you respect your space," Tom answered, "because it looks nice. Respect your discipline." He added, "Circus skills are just one part of it. You have to have respect for the show, respect for everything you do."

Jessica required every Arch to contribute ten hours per month of community service to the circus, so Iking had done his share of washing dishes. But Tom's messages resonated with him in a deeper, more mature way. "When people tell me the right thing," he said, "I be listening."

Iking became accustomed to arriving hours ahead of class time to clean—not to check off compulsory chores but to carry out self-imposed responsibilities. After he was satisfied that he'd done a good job, he trained. He made grueling physical and mental demands of himself and determined to meet them.

Over time, the combination and the intensity of these activities had an impact on Iking. "I changed the way I look at life because of the audition," he said. Before this audition, I did not respect the circus as much. I didn't care about things so much."

ENC accepted his written application, and by the time he flew to Montreal for his live audition in February 2011, he said, "I achieved most of the goals."

The auditions started at 8:30 in the morning, ended at 10:00 at night, and lasted for four days. He acted, tumbled, improvised, clowned, danced, walked the tightwire, and did hand-to-hand acrobatics with T-Roc, who was also applying.

On April 1, Iking's phone rang. It was T-Roc. He had not been admitted. Iking felt terrible for him.

Iking had not received his own results because he didn't have e-mail. The school was to send its decision to Jessica, who hadn't contacted him yet. Fearing the worst, Iking called her. "I quit circus," he said. "I'm not coming back."

"I got the results," she said. "I'm sorry. You didn't make it."

Iking dropped to the floor.

"April Fool's!" Jessica yelled.

Iking was so relieved—he was accepted! Warren helped him fill out and submit the documents that Canada required of foreign students. Diane held a fund-raiser to help cover his tuition and living expenses in Montreal.

"What It's Like to Be Different"

When she became an Arch in the winter of 2010, Meghan was delighted to find that her training and classes would be free and she would be paid for appearing in shows. But she soon discovered that Jessica exacted a high price. "You devote your life!" Meghan said, "Give her your soul!"

In addition to their community service work, Arches had to go to class, rehearse, help with fund-raising, and perform at

*Meghan performs at the
Mongolian review*

City Museum and other venues a minimum of five times a week.
Meghan spent at least three hours there on Mondays, Thursdays,
and Fridays, six hours on Saturdays, and four hours on Sundays—
for a total of about twenty hours every week.

Time management became an issue. She woke up at 4:00 in
the morning to do her homework. Unlike her friends, she had no
time to cruise the internet or text. "I definitely lost out on a lot of
opportunities to be with my friends," she said. "I had a boyfriend,
and we broke up. I realized the relationships that I had with my
friends were more difficult than I thought because I was spending
so much time with circus."

When kids at school learned that she was in a circus, they'd say, "You're a freak." Unlike Shai, Meghan didn't like the label.

But her opportunities to display her skills, sometimes in unexpected places, outweighed the struggles. The Arches performed with the St. Louis Symphony during a concert at Powell Symphony Hall. Meghan opened the program. "That was one of the most amazing experiences I had with circus," she said. "I was the single spotlight. The rest of the stage was dark. And there was me…[before] an entire symphony orchestra…with tiers of people."

At a theater in Washington, DC, Meghan performed in a Mongolian cultural review that featured traditional dance, music, and circus arts. Rosa had arranged the event in memory of her husband and their son, both of whom had been famous musicians at home before they died. She attended a party at the Mongolian embassy afterward. "I was the only non-Mongolian," Meghan said. "We forget what it's like to be conscious of your race…. Being there made me realize what it's like to be different." In particular, she was taller than almost everyone else.

Even though Circus Harmony, the Arches, and her high school were all composed of a wide variety of people of different races, ethnicities, religions, ages, economic levels, talents, and abilities, Meghan hadn't noticed her own differentness until she was a minority of one.

"At the circus, there's always someone similar to you," she said, echoing Jessica, who focused on similarities rather than differences. "I'm not physically like them [Mongolians]. Yet, I'm doing something that's a part of their culture." This experience, along with her travels in Israel, affected Meghan's long-term plans.

After a year or so, Meghan found a balance among all of the demands and began to feel that "circus was my normal." Even Jessica's toughness didn't faze her. Jessica rarely complimented her elite troupers. "I expect people to do the right thing," Jessica explained. "Why should I praise you for doing what you should be doing?"

Meghan took this approach in stride and thrived under Jessica and Rosa's high standards. During her senior year of high school, she decided to expand her skills and commit even more time to circus. She worked on cradle and ladder routines with Keaton and on trapeze with Rosa. She, Keaton, and Kellin developed a popular show, which they put on at benefits and parties as often as twice a week.

"The three of us would do a lot of outside gigs because we work well together," Meghan said. "I did the contortion. Kellin

Meghan and Keaton perform in Tessitura

157

could do juggling. He and Keaton could switch off on stilts. And I could do acrobatics with Keaton. We could put together a pretty diverse show."

They worked well together until she and Keaton, whom she had been dating, broke up. "I was feeling very openly unwanted," Meghan said. She could trust Keaton not to drop her physically, but she was left out of decisions about how to create acts, which gigs to accept, and whom to feature. Even their salaries seemed inequitable to her, as Kellin and Keaton received higher pay.

"I learned a lot about gender roles through that experience," Meghan said. "Circus is very much a patriarchal society." She wondered whether she lost out because males, in general, have more power or because Keaton and Kellin were Jessica's children. Regardless, she stated, "I never got my way in any situation, whatsoever."

Meghan knew she wasn't the only Arch who was being ignored. "If I or Alex or Elliana or Shaina would have a suggestion to make transitions or make stylistic changes to improve the overall flow of the act, the ideas would either be immediately shut down or it would take three or four times of explaining before the group was willing to try the suggestion out. It was incredibly frustrating especially when other ideas put forth—usually by one of the guys—were tried right away."

Meghan wished she could talk with Jessica about these issues. If she had, Jessica might have pointed out that the guys had grown up in the circus; they were seniors while Meghan, who had signed up in middle school, was a novice. Since Meghan's parents weren't circus performers, she'd had a much later start. She felt that she could never catch up.

Jessica knew from her own experiences that some professional circuses stick to traditional roles for men and women while others are more open. "Men tend to do the rigging while women work on costumes and take care of the children," she said. "But women do amazing tricks and even have tiger acts." And of course, her company was run by a woman; and Jessica thought of herself as a feminist.

Meghan didn't dare raise these issues. Whether or not Jessica said so directly, "We were being told that, in the real world, [it] would not be socially acceptable to ask those kinds of questions." She remained distressed but polite.

"I'm on My Way to Being Good"

Alex sat on the bleachers and groaned. "Teachers are trying to pile on work," she said, "trying to get their last grades in before the break. And I'm thinking, *Tomorrow, I'm going to be at circus for four-and-a-half hours. I don't know how I'm going to get ten hours of work I need to get done.*"

Unlike Meghan, Alex chafed under the demands Jessica placed on the Arches' schedules. She was spending six days a week at circus. For a while, she tried to do homework during breaks at circus but soon gave up. The music, clattering equipment, and constant motion around her were too distracting. When faced with a conflict between circus and academics, she put school first.

"If I have to miss a practice for schoolwork, it doesn't bother me," she said. "It definitely bothers Jessica a lot. But it doesn't bother me. I'd much rather get behind here than get behind at school."

It had taken Alex years to learn to ignore Jessica's complaints about her priorities. In the fifth or sixth grade, she said, "I missed practice for Circus Harmony two days in a row because I had projects in school.... Because I hadn't given her an explanation that she considered adequate, she yelled at me in front of the entire aerial group, making accusations that I don't care about the circus."

When she was younger, Alex sometimes returned home from circus sobbing because of what she perceived as Jessica's borderline verbal abuse. Jessica, on the other hand, noticed that Alex was sometimes "present but not working" and at other times, AWOL. She talked with Alex's parents, who seemed to share her concerns.

Like Meghan, Alex also experienced social conflicts. "I've had to overcome always missing out," she said. "I'm consistently absent from my friends at school. It makes it difficult to maintain relationships outside of circus."

Still, she enjoyed circus, the tricks she was learning, and her relationships there. "If it upset me that much, I wouldn't have stayed in circus that long. And I've developed friendships here at circus too, so it's not like I'm missing it all."

Because of a knee injury, Alex decided to focus on hand balancing during her junior year in high school. "Hand balancing is a very frustrating act to work," Alex said, "because it takes a long time to get things that don't seem very difficult. Rosa initially taught me a splits hand stand. That's the easiest one because your legs also balance you, rather than just your hands."

*Alex practices hand balancing
with Rosa*

Once she could support her body weight on her hands and arms with her legs spread apart, she started working on a one-handed hand stand. Alex struggled even more to get this trick right, but she didn't mind. She took a critical view of her progress. "Frustrating processes…are the things that I enjoy doing…. I don't think of myself as being good. I'm on my way to being good," she said. "And once I'm good, I'll be on my way to being really good."

When she got to the point where she was advancing quickly in hand balancing, Alex almost came full circle. Rosa tried to convince her to move back to Russia, where she was born, so she could work with trainers for the Moscow Circus.

"Rosa thought it would be best for me…to learn from the best coaches in the world. I was actually considering it. We talked to my parents. We were really thinking about it and putting the details together. But I came to the conclusion…[that] none of that is what I want for my future."

After deliberating, she realized that, unlike Iking, she did not want to be a professional circus performer. She wanted to balance circus, friends, and school—even if Jessica thought her priorities were out of whack.

"We Need Criticism"

Just after school ended in May 2011, Shaina returned to St. Louis with her mother, who was recently divorced. "Jessica was one of the first people I called," Shaina said. "She was very excited to hear from me and to hear that I was…able to be back in circus."

Although Shaina had lived in Rock Island for six years, Alex said she didn't feel as if Shaina had been absent for long. Their friendship picked right up where it had left off.

To Shaina's disappointment, she wasn't ready to perform in Circus Flora that summer. But she immediately started as an assistant teacher in tumbling, mini-tramp, and object manipulation and took classes at Circus Harmony in acting, ballet, and everything that Rosa taught. She decided to focus on juggling and aerials, especially ladder. And there was a trick off of the mini-tramp that she really wanted to master.

Shaina agreed with Meghan about the value of having tough coaches. "We need criticism, and we need to know what we did wrong and what we need to fix," she said. "A lot of people weren't too happy that it's almost all criticism and no compliments, but I don't really mind that it's no compliments because it tells me that I need to do better. If [Jessica] gives a compliment then it means I've done really well."

Shaina felt that it was particularly important for her to focus on juggling. "It's not very usual in this circus for girls to juggle," she said, "and I just wanted to make it so it's both genders juggling."

But she felt at a standstill with her juggling skills, just as Kellin had. While she could now manage four balls and was approaching five, everyone else had improved in her absence. In particular, she felt insecure at passing clubs. So she concentrated on correcting her patterns and asked anyone who was available to practice with her. Within a month, she could pass well with a partner and could even toss clubs under her leg and while spinning around.

Shaina already had an aerial act, but she wanted to spark it up with more advanced tricks. It took several months but she

Shaina balances on a globe

161

finally reached her goals—a foot hang and a toe hang from the ladder and from a spinning trapeze.

She was especially pleased when she got a "full"—a complete rotation in midair—after springing off the mini-tramp. "It's the rotation part that's hard," she said, "not the height. I would get it every once in a while but it wasn't a solid trick." As with the foot and toe hangs, she needed several months of persistent practice.

By July 2011, Shaina had gotten back up to speed and was ready to perform at the UniverSOUL preshow during the St. Louis stop of its national tour.

Like Iking, Shaina respected circus as an enterprise. "Performing with any circus is a great experience, and it should be acknowledged at all times," she said.

She was especially thrilled and honored to appear with UniverSOUL because it was her favorite. The troupe includes many minority and international entertainers, and conveys a happy, boisterous, family-friendly atmosphere.

She was, however, a little nervous about the animals. As the Arches waited to go on, they stood beside the elephants and near the tiger cages. "It was really scary because elephants can kill you," Shaina said. "The ring crew gave us warnings. We can't run around the elephants or make loud noises." For the kids' safety, the crew also pushed the tiger cages farther away.

The Arches' energy, Shaina knew, was often contagious. "When I perform, I like to look at the audience," she said, "and see how they react to tricks we do. A lot of the audience members had a smile on their faces, and they were clapping with the music and dancing."

Shaina's living situation was still not happy though. When she and her mother returned to St. Louis in May, they moved in with Shaina's grandmother. With four or five adults and seven grandchildren in the two-bedroom household, Shaina had to sleep either on the couch or on the floor in the living room. She stashed her clothes in a basement storage area.

Even worse, her grandmother's neighborhood was unsafe. "There was a lot of abandoned houses on our street. There's a corner store," Shaina said, "and there was always some type of shooting…or somebody would try and rob the corner store. I was pretty scared…. I really wasn't allowed to be outside."

At the end of the summer, Shaina's mother moved to a friend's home. But Shaina didn't know her mother's friend or feel comfortable with her. At that point, the state of Missouri officially declared Shaina homeless, and Jessica invited her to stay with her. She could get rides to circus, and her school was near Jessica's house.

This arrangement worked well until Christmas Day 2011, when Shaina's mother got into an argument with her friend and moved back to her own mother's house. She made Shaina come too. Then her mother moved in with a boyfriend. This time, Shaina stayed with her grandmother.

The moves meant that Shaina had to switch to a charter school, her second high school that year. But until the arrangements could be made, she missed classes altogether for nearly three weeks. When Shaina was finally enrolled, she found that she didn't like the school because it was too easy. They didn't assign homework or give tests. "I don't think I learned very much," she said.

At the end of the academic year, the school board closed the charter school, and Shaina had to find another one to attend for her senior year. By then it wasn't clear that she could enroll anywhere as a senior because she had taken neither the required state tests in ninth and tenth grades nor the courses required to pass the tests in the eleventh grade.

With three different homes and three schools in two years, Shaina found a refuge in circus—friends she could trust and adults she could rely on. Although she didn't learn as much at school as she wished, her circus skills continued to improve and make her proud.

Galilee Arches?

By spring 2012, two years had passed since the Arches and the Galilee Circus had performed together. The members of both circuses had felt the benefits of their joint journeys in 2007 and 2008, and Jessica had hoped that they would exchange visits annually. She had tried to make that happen back in 2009, when it would have been the Arches' turn to return to Israel. Marc would have been happy to welcome them but the Galilee Foundation for Value Education couldn't foot the bill, and Jessica's board of directors opposed her efforts to raise the money needed for yet another international trip so soon. So Jessica compromised on biannual visits—alternating between St. Louis and the Galilee.

That agreement didn't guarantee that her board would be enthusiastic about spearheading another fund-raising campaign. Despite the benefits, it would be not only expensive but also complicated.

None of these obstacles deterred Jessica from proceeding. "Oh, I just decided that it's going to happen, no matter what," Jessica said. "That's what I've done every time, even though, as we get close, we sometimes don't have [the money]."

As usual, the prospects for a trip in 2012 did not look good.

Chapter Twelve

THE GALILEE CIRCUS: FLYING SOLO 2012

In February 2012, an interfaith group of ministers, preachers, and rabbis from Philadelphia traveled to Israel, where they caught a performance by the Galilee Circus. They were charmed. Talking with the visitors afterward, Marc mentioned that the troupers hoped to go to St. Louis the following summer. One of the ministers asked Marc, "Could you stop in Philly?"

Marc answered, "If you can raise the money for the difference in airfare, that would be great."

Marc let Jessica know that if she could raise the funds for the overseas portion of the trip, as well as scrounge housing and meals in St. Louis, then the Galilee Circus would be able to tack a side trip to Philadelphia onto their itinerary. This meant that the group would perform not just at festivals, schools, and hospitals near home but also before audiences 6,000 miles away. By themselves. Without the famed St. Louis Arches to prop them up. The Galilee Circus could embark on its own international tour.

Marc and Dagan couldn't tell the kids, since Jessica had barely begun to raise the money. "The uncertainty followed us all year long," Dagan said.

While the adults were feeling stressed about the trip, the troupers faced a different challenge—an entirely new kind of performance. Some of them fretted that an ambitious production would dissolve into disaster.

"Circus is about expressing how we're capable of extraordinary things...."

—Marc Miller

Entrance to the gym at Biane

Dream On

"There's two kinds of shows," Roey explained. "There's the kind of show…which is built out of acts…. Just take all kinds of acts and put them together." That's the sort of program that the Galilee Arches shuffled together when the Galilee Circus and the St. Louis Arches combined forces.

"The other kind," Roey went on, "is an actual show, with a story…" The Arches' annual shows—*Espressivo, Café Appassionato, Tessitura*—represented a limited version of this kind of show. Each had a distinct theme. Costumes, music, sets, ringmaster patter, and tricks were designed to match. These shows set a context for a story but didn't contain a plot.

The Galilee Circus had never attempted a sophisticated production of this kind; they had never even thought about it until Veronika worked with them. She thought that they could—and should—pull off not just an Arches-type revue, but a show that told a story. They had some very advanced technical circus skills, she noticed, but no theatrical training. "This made them look…more like a sports club than a circus," Veronika said.

Talking with her about the origins and development of circus, Marc came to a realization, "The American [circus] tradition… is primarily a demonstration of skills and prowess. The European tradition…puts a higher value on clowning, drama, plot, emotions. While there are elements of this in Jessica's circus's annual shows, our contact with them has included almost none of this. We learned from them skills, strength, and presentation—no clowning at all, for example. I had been feeling for a long time that the dramatic element was lacking in our circus."

To stage such a show, the Galilee Circus had to learn to improvise, act, pantomime, and clown. In particular, Veronika taught them to make big, loose gestures. For this kind of exuberant presentation, they must definitely not stand stiffly with their arms behind their backs between tricks or style, like the St. Louis Arches.

With her guidance, the Galileans crafted a melodramatic

mystery tale with a plot, characters, a stage set, music, conflict, humor, pathos, suspense, and a moral. Because Veronika had to return to Germany every three months to retain her visa, responsibility for expanding the basic script, rehearsing, and mounting the show became a communal effort.

The Galileans helped develop the storyline and created the visual gags. They found and recorded music appropriate for each scene, made or scrounged their own costumes, built the scenery from boxes and stray lumber, and rigged special lighting. Then they advertised the show in the Karmiel newspaper.

Throughout February and March, Roey warned, "We're not going to make it. We can't make a show under pressure. You can't schedule a show until you have a show!"

Mishaps, distractions, and aggravations abounded. Shai proposed revisions to the plot so incessantly—"like a bubbling fountain," Veronika said—that he unnerved the rest of the cast. Hala insisted on trying to balance on the rolla bolla, even though her skills were not strong. Roey struggled to overcome his shyness. Hla, the only contortionist, had earned a trip to the United States because of her exemplary grades in English class and did not participate in the show at all.

The Galilee Circus rehearses
Dream On

The hour-long pantomime circus-play was never officially titled. Some kids referred to it as *The Galilee Restaurant Show.* Shai dubbed it *Dream On.*

Ahmed took the leading role, playing a server in a restaurant. In the play his boss, Ali, abuses him. After Ali leaves for the night, Ahmed falls asleep. He dreams that he is the boss, and Ali is the servant. During Ahmed's dream, A Very Important Customer, played by Shai, unicycles into the restaurant, juggling a hat and cane. Hala, as a waitress, turns the table decorations—a vase and a serving tray—into a rolla bolla, on which she rocks back and forth as she takes his order.

After the intermission, the story takes a dark and mysterious turn. Shai steals money from the cash register and flees the

Shirel spotlights Shai from the trapeze

restaurant. While searching for him, Roey, Ahmed, Ali, Samer Sanallah, and Saeed Assaf tumble and do acrobatics. The girls, including Hala and Shirel, climb high on silks and trapeze to spot the criminal. After luring Shai from his hiding place—in the audience—Ahmed is declared a hero and makes Shai wash the dishes. Until, that is, the real Ali returns and wakes up Ahmed, who, once again, becomes the restaurant's servant.

Dozens of Arabs and Jews came together to watch the show in the gym in Biane, and they whistled, applauded, and cheered their approval. "They don't even notice the villain sitting right next to them," Shai said, "because they're so mesmerized by circus."

"It was the best show we ever did," Roey said.

"You Are Unrelenting"

Jessica had begged her board of directors to help raise money for the Israelis' visit, but they weren't taking action. So she kicked off an online campaign through Kickstarter.

"My board of directors was furious at me for that," Jessica said, "furious that I had put [a goal of $20,000] on there, that I had done Kickstarter at all, that I had put such a high number that they thought was unattainable."

The problem, her board discovered, was that, unlike some other social-media platforms, Kickstarter requires that all of the requested money be raised by a specified deadline. If it is not, then none of the money that people pledge through its website is actually donated to the organization. If the total amount pledged reached only $19,999, Circus Harmony would not be able to collect any of it. Jessica had not realized that. "I don't always read the fine print," she admitted.

She hoped that the Galilee Circus would be able to pay the airfare for its troupers and staff members but Marc reminded her that, given the incomes of most of the circus families, that was not possible. She then suggested that the kids hold car washes to raise money. But Marc explained that a car wash would seem like an alien idea in Israel. Kids don't hold that kind of fund-raiser there and cars generally remain dusty. The Galileans did put on a show to raise money but they didn't make much. Again, Marc proposed waiting another year to visit.

"Oh, no," Jessica insisted. "You're coming."

Marc responded, "You are unrelenting."

In mid-April, Jessica announced her Kickstarter goal: $20,000 by 6:36 p.m. on June 15. "We started to whisper to each other that we might go to America." Hala said. At the end of May, however, with only two weeks remaining before the deadline, Jessica still had to raise nearly $15,000. Even though the interfaith groups in Philadelphia were expecting the Galilee Circus to arrive in six weeks, Marc couldn't make plane reservations because he didn't have the money in hand to pay for them.

The Israeli rumor mill switched directions. "Ahmad told all the kids that there's a big chance that we might not be going," Hala said. She had never been on a plane or outside of Israel. "I was stressed because I really wanted to go.... And, it might be ruined."

Meanwhile, the Arches pitched in. "We did a lot of shows that helped fund-raise for the Galilee Circus to get to St. Louis." Shaina said. "We also helped get food." Meghan organized a car wash, since the Israelis couldn't. They held an event at a bookstore, which donated a portion of sales to the cause.

After those successes, Roey's mother told him, "You might be going." But he knew he shouldn't tell the others, in case the Americans couldn't come up with the rest of the cash.

During the final week of the campaign, Jessica posted more and more frantic pleas.

> *Be like Peter Pan and help our children fly!*
> *We're squeezed.*
> *Donate something.*
> *We need you.*

With one day to spare, Jessica crawled across the finish line. In fact, she raised $21,716. The Galilee Circus was going to America, after all—and not just to St. Louis, but to Philadelphia as well.

"We Have to Make a Show!"

Again, there was a problem with the timing of the trip. It was scheduled during Ramadan, when the Muslim performers would be fasting. How could they manage to travel, rehearse, and perform—and not eat between sunup and sundown? Fortunately, Marc learned, there is a rule that allows observant Muslims to postpone fasting if it is impossible to abide by the usual requirements that month. They could tack on fasting days after the official end of Ramadan when they returned to Israel.

With just a month before departure, Marc, Dagan, and Ahmad discussed which troupers would make the trip. Marc asked the parents if they could each contribute $400 for incidentals. One Jewish family couldn't afford it, so two Arab families chipped in extra money. All of those who had participated in the 2010 Galilee Arches tour of Israel, including Hala, Roey, and Shai, were invited back. There were slots for a few more kids as well. The leaders wanted the group to consist of a mixed but balanced group of six Arabs and six Jews.

When Ahmad told Hla that she could join the group, she thought he was kidding. "I didn't take it seriously," she said.

A week later, Hla discovered that he'd meant what he said. She showed up late for a practice and saw that the group that was going to America was holding a meeting.

"What's going on?" she asked.

"We're going to the USA," someone said, "and you are going with us."

Hla blinked. "I'm going to the USA?"

"Yes!"

"I was really astonished," she admitted.

In addition to discussing logistics, including arrangements for passports and visas, Dagan told the troupers, "We have to make a show and make it as good as it can be." They had barely four weeks to shine up their acts.

Hala and Einat focused on silks. Roey still wanted desperately to get round-off back tucks. "I practiced it all the year,"

Hala performs silks

Members of the Galilee Circus practice back bends

he said, "but when the rumor started that we were going, I really… put all my efforts in it."

Hla and Meghan had become Facebook friends. Between the messages from Meghan and the videos and photographs of Circus Harmony that Jessica posted, Hla could see exactly what Meghan was working on. And that's what Hla wanted to learn. Since she didn't have a dedicated contortion coach like Rosa to teach her, Hla peered at her computer screen.

"I was practicing hard," Hla said. "I wanted to do those things, like hand standing. I wanted to do what Meghan do and more…. I observed them deeply."

Shai hoped that the trip would help him professionally. "Once we knew we were going to America," he said, "that was the time when I started to think about going to circus school. Jessica's opinion meant a lot to me because she knows about circus schools…. I wanted to work with Richard and their clowning teacher."

The Galileans had a lot at stake. At least one trouper felt ready to go. Days before their departure, Roey finally got his back tuck—just as he had achieved three diabolos before their last trip!

Philadelphia!

A two-hour train ride to Tel Aviv and an eleven-hour flight later, the Galileans landed in Philadelphia, where they were scheduled to put on a show at a gymnastics facility that very day.

But Einat didn't emerge from Passport Control with everyone else. An officer had pulled her aside for questioning. A native Spanish-speaker and recent Hebrew-learner, Einat had to try to understand him and explain herself in English.

Her visa was pasted inside her old Mexican passport, which had expired. Why was she carrying an expired passport? the officer wanted to know. Why was her visa in that passport? Why did she also have an Israeli passport? Why was she in America, anyway? Yes, she could leave Israel, they told her—no problem. But, no, she could not enter the United States. She'd have to take the next flight back to Tel Aviv, at her own expense, by herself.

Einat was nearly in tears. Then she realized that the officers were Hispanic. She switched to Spanish and quickly persuaded them to let her in. Beaming, she emerged from Passport Control into steaming, sticky Philadelphia. *Sababa!* To celebrate, the Galileans formed a Pyramid in the airport's arrival hall.

Six hours later, the Galilee Circus put on its first show in Philadelphia.

"The show was terrible," Shai confessed. "We were yelling at each other. Mostly me. I was yelling." Everyone was tired. The sound system didn't work. The routines didn't flow smoothly. Shai dropped hats. Roey dropped diabolos.

But they finished the show. They met their host families, ate, slept, and perked up the next day when they were scheduled to perform at a day camp and a synagogue.

The Galilee Circus performing group had been developing, improving, and showing off their tricks for several years. By now, they had standard routines, which they pulled off reliably and impressively as long as they weren't tired and hungry and Shai didn't yell at them.

But something special happened that day in Philadelphia, when their enthusiasm and skills propelled them to a new level of showmanship. Standing in the middle of a gym floor at a community center, Roey spontaneously asked for a volunteer from the audience. "We always improvised the tricks," Roey said, "but not with the audience." Until that show in Philadelphia.

Roey motioned for a father and his two sons to come up. He lined them up between himself and Yaron, who assured the volunteers that he'd never hit anyone in the head before. The family stood as still and straight as doors while the jugglers passed the first set of clubs around them. Immediately, Yaron dropped one. The man's jaw clenched nervously, and the audience laughed.

Roey and Yaron juggle around an anxious father and his sons

Usually when circus performers talk about trust, they refer to the trust that they have in themselves and in their partners to, say, catch each other. In Philadelphia, Roey and Yaron put an entirely new spin on this idea. They asked the audience to trust them as well.

They discovered that they could be freer and looser in the U.S. than they were back home. At a synagogue, they made spontaneous jokes about large Jewish noses. The audience howled.

"You need to adapt your improvisation to each place," Roey later said. "We always think of different stuff to do."

Dave Gillies, a longtime professional juggler and coach in Philadelphia, watched them work. "It's not all about technique—and they had very nice moves," he said. "It's also about presence and interaction with the audience." Roey and Yaron demonstrated those with verve. Dave was so impressed with Shai's hat juggling that he videoed the act to show his students.

"I had pretty low expectations of what kids could do," one observer admitted. "They were doing great things!"

Their most significant endorsement came from Marc Miller, the managing director of the Philadelphia School of Circus Arts. He watched Roey pop onto Ali's shoulders. A Two-High—Miller's students could do that. Then, he saw Ahmed clamber up behind

Roey and, amazingly, pop up to Roey's shoulders. "A Three-High!" Miller exclaimed. "That's a pretty big accomplishment, to do that...and do tricks from that position. That's something that we can't do."

Miller was especially taken by the acrobats' fearlessness. "They're good tumblers, good jugglers, good on the unicycle," he said, "and are able to make you feel that sense of danger, which is not easy to do." The Galileans had succeeded in the essential challenge.

"Circus," Miller said, "is about expressing how we're capable of extraordinary things.... That is circus at its core—to illustrate that things that do not look possible...are very possible."

Over the past five years, these troupers had progressed from learning what to do with their bodies to knowing what their bodies were capable of doing. By the time the Galilee Circus left Philadelphia—after four days, four shows, and two workshops in acrobatics, aerials, silks, and gymnastics—they felt like true pros.

"We always felt the show we put together with the Arches is great because of the Arches." Roey said. "Philadelphia was the first time that we really felt proud of ourselves,"

Marc credited Dagan with improving the program. "He's grown up...in the job," Marc said. "He's got a circus there."

They were eager to join the Arches in St. Louis where, for the first time, Shai said, they would be "equal partners."

Twenty-three kids—six blacks and five whites from America, plus six Muslims and six Jews from Israel—walked out of the airport into St. Louis's 108-degree swelter.

Nearly a dozen of them had little idea what acts they would perform or with whom. Half of each group had never met members of the other group. Shaina had not seen the Israelis since she'd moved to Illinois, six years earlier.

As the two groups once again merged into the Galilee Arches, the troupers needed to form new teams and create joint acts quickly. In less than three days, they were to perform for UniverSOUL. The large and boisterous audience would have high expectations.

Combining Forces

This is my contortion girl! That was Hla's first thought the moment she saw Meghan.

Even though Meghan had accompanied the Arches to Israel in 2010, the two contortionists hadn't met. Hla had been too young and inexperienced to join that tour.

After following Meghan on Facebook for a year, she was now following her every move. "I really wanted to be her partner," Hla said. "I wanted to do a Meghan-and-I show!"

"Circus is really a different world."

—Hala Asadi

A Galilee Arches Pyramid

Roey and Shai looked forward to partnering with Kellin for juggling and with Keaton for acrobatics and tumbling, especially now that Roey had his round-off back tuck. Hala had been working hard on silks and wondered what tricks she could perform with the Arches.

Shaina could juggle rings, clubs, knives, and up to four balls, although she found the technique boring. She could also tumble, do acrobatics, and walk on stilts. Alex could tumble and do acrobatics, as well as fly on trapeze. With so many skills, they could match up with a number of the kids from the Galilee. How would they work it out?

First, they all convened at Jessica's house for a celebratory reunion dinner. Shaina noticed that Hala and Hla were standing together, but away from the others. "It seemed like no one wanted to talk to them, so I went over," she said. "The first thing we talked about was my trip to Israel…. Hala said she was Manar and Manal's sister. That's how I remembered her because I went to her party and stayed at her house."

The Israeli girls bunked down at Jessica's, while the guys headed off with other circus families for home stays. They all set up shop early the next morning, but not to plan their show. First, they were interviewed by a local television station.

As Marc and Jessica explained the multicultural, multi-ethnic, multiracial, multifaith, and multilingual makeup of their multitalented circuses, the camera panned across the kids. Roey, Yaron, and Lil Donald did diabolo. Kellin juggled clubs, and Shai unicycled and juggled hats. Hla and Meghan practiced a brand-new trick. Einat, Shirel, and Meghan showed off Split Spin with Keaton, Max, and Reggie Moore.

Marc concluded the interview by saying, "You've really got to trust the other person and not think about who he is or what language he speaks." At that moment, the camera captured the newly reconstituted Galilee Arches in its first, slightly shaky, Pyramid.

"No Playing Around"

Circus Harmony's ring was filled with summer campers, so after the interview, the troupes went to a large inner-city gym to concoct their show. For the first time in their five-year history together, the Israelis joined the Arches as peers. Following each of the three previous visits, the Galileans had mimicked some of the Arches' tricks as best they could and inserted them into their routines. This time, they brought their own tricks as well.

"We're taking two acts that already exist and putting everything together," Roey said.

The Galileans now knew how to work hard—and did. "Everybody's really focused and wants to succeed," Roey said. "So everybody's really doing exactly what they need to do, no playing around."

Actually, Hla and Meghan put their act together by doing just that—playing around and stretching out together. Although Hla had been keeping tabs on Meghan, Meghan didn't know what Hla could do. Watching each other gave them ideas. "She wasn't as flexible as I was or as cognizant of toes and knees and where your hands should go," Meghan said. "But at the same time, she did really well."

The first trick they developed together, called Nothing But Net, turned out to be their favorite. "That's where we're both standing," Meghan explained, "and we latch opposite hands with one another. Then, with our free hand…we would grab our leg of choice and bring it up over our heads. Then, we'd have two of the guys do a dive roll through our leg."

The diabolo jugglers also quickly combined forces. Roey and Yaron showed Lil Donald, Chauncey Kroner, and Miles Kroner their tricks, and then the Americans did the same. "We just took their act and our act and put them together," Roey said. Each juggling team learned the other's routines. The merged ensemble became known as the Debonair Diabolo Dudes. For ball and club juggling, they pulled in Max, Keaton, Reggie, Shai—and Shaina, the only female in the act.

Alex Wallenda coaches Shai on tightwire

177

"We all knew what we were going to do," Shai said. "We just switched partners." What a difference five years had made.

Meanwhile, Alex and Shirel choreographed a joint trapeze act. Both of them not only specialized in aerials, but were also Spanish speakers. They quickly discovered that they could communicate best with each other in Spanish. "We both sat down and watched each other's acts," Alex said, "and then we told each other exactly what we were willing to take out of our acts and what we weren't willing.… She does a lot of tricks that I've never learned, and so do I for her. So we took the tricks that both of us know and put it into a simple act." Each also built a short solo into their routine, so Shirel could show off her flowing moves and Alex could demonstrate her spicy drops.

The acts that took the longest to plan were acrobatics and charivari. Those acts took more time because everyone participated in both of them.

Charivari—the introductory teaser that allows every performer to flaunt a fragment of what she or he does best—was not only time-consuming, it was complex to orchestrate. A large number of people and objects—two circuses' worth—rolled, bounced, leaped, and flew around each other in Circus Harmony's small ring, and not, they hoped, into the audience, the glass windows, or each other. But since it was brief and packed with self-selected solos, charivari was less challenging for the performers than acrobatics.

From their first encounter with the Arches, the Galilee Circus had been dazzled by the Americans' acrobatics and tumbling. Many of the Arches were still more advanced than the Israelis. Nevertheless, every one of the Israelis was to participate in this part of the circus show.

But right out of the chute, the Galilee Arches suffered two injuries. Ali twisted his wrist when he landed wrong during a dive roll. And Roey flubbed a round-off back tuck and broke his finger. He decided not to tell his parents.

List of acts in Hebrew and English on the Circus Harmony chalkboard

In the afternoon, the troupers showed each other their tricks, both the new, combined ones and the older, established ones. They also ran them by Jessica and Dagan, who gave them four thumbs-up. Then they had to figure out the order of the acts and whether to walk, run, dive-roll, cartwheel, or back-flip into and out of the ring. They jotted the list in English and Hebrew on Circus Harmony's blackboard.

After sharing their tricks with kids at the Center's summer camp that afternoon, attending a Cardinals–Dodgers baseball game in the evening, and teaching a daylong workshop to campers at a local synagogue the following day, it was showtime. And this was just their third day together.

"Circus Is Really a Different World"

The Galilee Arches were scheduled to perform with UniverSOUL Circus early in their St. Louis tour. Although they had only a six-minute time slot, it was a high point for kids in both troupes, especially Shaina. The year before, she had felt honored to perform with her favorite circus. This year, it became her career goal. "I would like, one day, to be in UniverSOUL Circus," she said.

Even unloading their equipment and lugging it into the tent was exciting. Inside, the ring was spacious enough to hold, as the troupers soon saw, a pair each of camels, llamas, miniature horses, and zebras. Seats for more than 2,000 fans rose in tiers surrounding the ring.

Half a dozen reverberating speakers blasted hip-hop, pop, gospel, and soul music. Red, white, and blue lights swept back and forth across the darkened arena. A gigantic electronic wall flashed images of colorfully decorated, way-bigger-than-life-size faces alongside the circus's logo and motto—CircUS.

Meghan had also performed with UniverSOUL last year. Even though she was not planning a circus career, she was excited. "It's always fun to be in a tent, with a real ring," she said, "with lights and loud music and a crowd…with real rigging and tech and all those different theatrical aspects that you don't worry about when you're street performing."

All of this hoopla ratcheted up Meghan's resolve to do her best for the audience. "You always have this extra sense of confidence…. It makes you feel good about your work and what you're doing," she said.

Not that she didn't get nervous before blockbusters like this one. She did. "But when you get more anxious, it shows how much

The Galilee Arches unload their equipment at UniverSOUL Circus

you care.… If I'm not anxious about it, it no longer becomes a big deal. And you always want your performance to be a big deal."

Backstage, the Galilee Arches gathered with UniverSOUL's traveling cast and crew. They put on their costumes between the cast's caravans and the tiger cages and stepped aside to let the elephants lumber by.

For many of the Israelis, who had never set foot inside a circus tent, this behind-the-scenes experience felt almost otherworldly. "I was going into another life." Shirel said, "I could see how the life is for the people who live in the circus.… I saw one of the performers with a little boy, his child. It looked amazing!"

Kellin and his brother and sister already had a sense of this lifestyle. They had grown up in a circus, even though they hadn't ridden a circuit, as their mother had. Keaton and Elliana were already moving into it. Keaton was about to join Iking in Montreal at ENC. Elliana had recently returned home after a year at *l'École de cirque de Québec* and was now pondering her next move.

"Circus is really a different world," Hala said, "but for the people who are inside, not outside. The people who are inside the circus, we have some sort of bonding…having fun, playing, practicing, having shows."

Israeli Arabs and Jews who are on the outside can't have such fun together. Or at least they aren't aware that they can. They're not even aware of what fun they're missing. They'd have to run away to the circus (or to one of the other established coexistence projects) to find out that maybe they too could get along with each other, if they wanted to.

"They Felt Comfortable"

A half-dozen Galilee Arches burst from the chute into the brightly lit ring and unfurled their red mats. Shaina and others quickly taped them down flat, then rejoined the rest of the troupe and ran in concentric circles, waving at the audience as they performed dive rolls, cartwheels, front and back flips—every move in their repertoire.

*Shaina and the Galilee Arches
at UniverSOUL Circus*

"It felt funner on stage with them [the Israelis]," Kellin said. "They felt comfortable."

The crowd was especially enthusiastic when Kellin, Chauncey, Lil Donald, and Max made—and then corrected—a mistake. The trick was a dramatic one. Chauncey popped onto Max's shoulders, and Lil Donald onto Kellin's. At the same time that Lil Donald back-flipped from Kellin's shoulders onto a mat, Chauncey was supposed to back-flip from Max's shoulders to Kellin's. But Chauncey missed and fell. The audience started to clap anyway. Max held up a finger to let them know they'd do it again—this time the right way. And they did.

Of course, the Galilee Arches polished off their fast-paced teamwork with a traditional final Pyramid before tumbling out of the ring.

THE GALILEE ARCHES 2012

Knowing Shaina's career dreams, the troupe had made a plan to help her impress UniverSOUL's director. "They made a group decision on letting me tumble out last," Shaina said, "because I was the best female tumbler. I had talked to the man who hires acts.… They decided to let me tumble out last so the man can see how great I was and how graceful I could be."

Shaina was remarkably graceful, given the pain she was suffering. "At the very beginning of the act, I was popping up to [Max's] shoulders, and the timing was off. He went up when I went down, and it messed up my knee." This was the knee that she had injured in Rock Island. "But I still performed as if it didn't hurt, even though it did." It hurt so much that she was crying. Alex discreetly carried her out of the ring at the end of the act.

The circus director came backstage to talk with Shaina after the show. He wanted to make sure she was all right. She was touched by his concern—and pleased that she had made an impression on him.

"They Had Amazing Teachers"

The Galilee Arches settled into City Museum for several days of coaching, rehearsals, and shows. Their schedules were packed so tight that they had less time for training than they had hoped.

Shai barely had time to talk with Jessica and Richard. "Everything was scheduled. We had lots of shows, lots of rehearsals," Shai complained. "We were told what to do in our free time.… They had amazing teachers I wanted to work with—Richard—a lot more than I did. I only had a few minutes with him.… That was a disappointment. I wanted to work and practice." Still, when Richard watched Shai's hat act, he called it "world class!"

"We should be warming up right now!" Hla kept urging Meghan. "Let's get to the ring!"

"Hla was so happy to learn and to work that it was fun," Meghan said. "She was making sure that I was always on point, being ready!" *Mishmaa'at!*

Even more importantly, Hla had the chance to work with Rosa. "Rosa is the top!" she exclaimed.

Right away, Hla noticed differences in the ways that Rosa and Leonid taught contortion. First Rosa stretched Hla, Hala, and the other girls in completely new ways. She had them place one heel on the seat of a chair and stretch their other leg behind them on the floor; then they did it on the other side, with the opposite foot on the chair. These, Hla learned, were called stretch-over splits.

"If you're close to having your splits but you're not quite there," Meghan explained, "the ground is preventing you from pushing all the way down. It's giving you a means of pushing up.... When you put your leg up on the chair, there's an extra [distance] that you have to go to be on the ground. You have a lot more room to sink down."

The Israelis worked hard on sinking. Hala knelt on the floor, propped her back foot on a chair, and touched the back of her head to that foot. Hla lay on Rosa's lap, her torso facing Rosa's legs, her legs behind Rosa's arms, and her feet on Rosa's shoulders. She leaned back and clasped her hands behind Rosa's neck, while Rosa gently but persistently pushed Hla's torso forward.

"Everything is different," Hla said. "She focused on how to make it the correct way with the most stability of the limbs, how to move the legs without pain." Although the girls winced and sometimes moaned each time Rosa pushed their hips down another half inch, straightened their shoulders, or pressed the tops of their feet flat on the floor, they claimed that the maneuvers didn't hurt. In the end, they laughed in disbelief at how much farther they could stretch and contort their bodies.

"Leonid gave us the opportunity to make the splits," Hla said. "Then he hangs around with us and looks. If he sees something wrong, he corrects it."

Shai felt that Leonid made less effort to teach than the American coaches did. "He would just...tell us what to do, and he wouldn't give us feedback or tips."

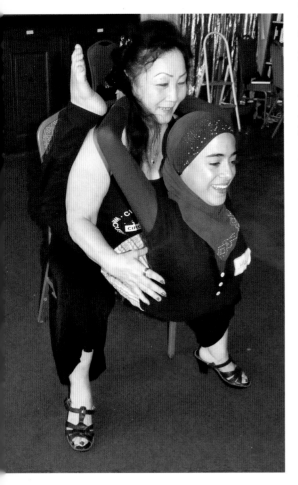

Rosa stretches Hla

This was the common Israeli way of coaching students. Dagan explained the reason for this approach. "I give them the basic training.… I don't want to tell them what to do. I just want to support them and follow them, not them follow me. It's a youth circus; it's not a professional circus."

Many kids in the Galilee Circus now questioned this attitude. They knew they were ready to go pro—perhaps not for their careers, but as paid performers for local productions back home. Although everyone recognized how far they'd come under Dagan's leadership, they felt frustrated at his casual style.

Hla noticed another advantage of working with Rosa. She specialized in females. Hla felt that Rosa's approach worked best for her, though she had learned a great deal from Leonid, from her own individual practice, and from studying Meghan on Facebook and YouTube.

Hla and Hala quickly adopted tricks they learned from Rosa, Alex, and Meghan. And Hla got her wish: she became Meghan's Galilee Arches partner.

Because of their shared love for aerials, Alex and Shirel worked together. Throughout the spring, Shirel had been determined to reach three goals before coming to America. She wanted to juggle three balls—check. Do a back flip—check. And make drops on the trapeze—nope, not yet. That's where Alex helped. "She taught me to stand up in the trapeze, and then we go, like, falling but then catch ourselves with our leg, with one knee and the other knee out straight and pointed. It took just two times to learn."

Alex could do the drop faster, so they worked out a way to take turns during performances. Each girl styled and gestured toward the other while she performed her specialty. "The audience saw she was as good as me," Alex said, "but different."

Alex also taught Shirel to hang from the trapeze by her feet, a trick she'd tried but never mastered in Israel. Alex positioned Shirel and held her until she got it right. Shirel was proud when Alex stood back, looked at her, and announced, "Good!"

Diversions

"I loved going to the zoo with the Israelis!" Alex said. "In circus, you're kind of like an animal in the zoo. You're being watched, and people don't treat you like a human."

For the first time, Shai noticed certain aspects of American culture. "Everything is commercialized. There's commercials everywhere," he said. He laughed about a St. Louis radio show called *Free Twelve*, which guaranteed twelve minutes of programming with no advertisements. "Here [in Israel], you only have two channels with commercials on TV."

The troupers returned to Trout Lodge, a YMCA camp where they had also stayed for several days in 2008. The staff was amazed by the teens' climbing abilities on the alpine equipment. The Americans were intrigued that Hla wore a full body-covering suit, complete with hijab, to swim. Afterward she dried her clothing—which she was still wearing—with a hair dryer.

The Israelis were especially enthusiastic about an excursion to a shopping mall. During their performance there, a group of girls in hijab gathered nearby. They were Palestinians from the West Bank, who were visiting relatives in St. Louis. The Arabic speakers had a good time chatting with each other.

Because the Muslims in the circus were unable to observe Ramadan, Jessica arranged a visit to Daar Ul Islam, a local mosque. Several of the girls were menstruating, and decided not to attend. The American mosque, like others in the United States, allows women and girls to pray there while they have their periods, but Hla and Hala were uncomfortable doing so, since the custom is different in Deir al-Asad.

Instead, all of the girls hung out at Meghan's house where they watched the Olympics on television and danced. Hla and Hala felt free not only to join in—something they would not do in front of boys—but even to do "dirty dancing." Alex admitted, "We were all shocked."

The service at Daar Ul Islam was read from the Qur'an, as is traditional, but the mosque's members, who came mostly from

Hla and Hala meet Muslim girls at the mall

Pakistan and India, did not speak Arabic. This surprised and disappointed the Muslim members of the circus who had hoped to talk with other Arabic speakers. As in Israel, the women prayed separately upstairs (as do Jewish women in orthodox synagogues). After the service, the members invited everyone to share in the communal *iftar*, the end-of-day meal that breaks the daily fast during Ramadan.

The members of Daar Ul Islam knew that Jews would attend the *iftar*, so they arranged for kosher meals for them. Coincidentally, it was also *Tisha b'Av*, a Jewish holiday, so Marc was fasting too. During his nearly three weeks in the United States that summer, one of the few specially prepared kosher meals he ate was at the mosque. The rabbi and the Muslims broke their fasts together that night. After dinner, the jugglers gave an impromptu demonstration and workshop in the mosque's courtyard.

"Get Your Woman Back"

In the blog he posted for troupers' families back in Israel, Marc commented that "these guys held on without a hitch…disciplined, well behaved, and bonded." That assessment was largely true. There were, however, a couple of glitches that had ethnic overtones.

Hala and Hla went for a walk around Jessica's neighborhood and inadvertently left the back door open. Her dog came inside and pooped in the room where the girls' beds and sleeping bags were set up. "It's because of you that the door was open and the dog pooped," Shirel told Hala and Hla. "So, you should clean it."

The cousins denied that they were responsible and refused to help. Hala later recalled that Shirel yelled at them, "Why don't you clean? You Arabs don't clean. You're so messy, you don't care! You're dirty." (Shirel remembers accusing Hala and Hla—but not all Arabs—of being messy and irresponsible.)

The three girls shouted at one another. Hla cried. Alex said, "Even with the circus keeping us all together, there was still that segregation between the two cultures."

The next day, Alex stepped between Roey and Ali just as a disagreement was about to turn into a shoving match. She heard Ali tell Roey, "Get your woman back." Alex interpreted his demand as "Put her in her place." She was surprised and disturbed by Ali's perception of women as men's possessions. Roey understood how Alex felt and defused the situation, saying to her, "We should go."

Events like these gave both the Israelis and the Americans perspectives on their own and each other's cultures. The hard feelings dissolved, and everyone performed together as usual the next day. In fact, just a short time later they all sang "Happy Birthday!" to Roey in three languages.

Showtime!

The thoroughly merged Galilee Arches troupers threw themselves into their last performance at City Museum with extra vigor. Despite his broken finger, Roey pulled off a series of back handsprings

Shirel and Alex perform trapeze

while Yaron spun a diabolo beneath him, a feat that required milli-second timing. Then Roey performed his tour de force—three dia-bolos cascading on, off, and back on the string, over and under his raised leg. He also took Keaton's place, diving through Hla's leg in Nothing But Net. Hla and Meghan intertwined and twisted grace-fully before prancing from the ring holding hands.

Alex and Shirel stood on the trapeze bar, grinned at each other—and then plunged. Someone in the audience screamed. Before the scream died out—and before the aerialists crashed onto the ring's red carpet—each girl jerked herself to a halt by catching the bar with one knee.

Everyone who could juggle did. Shai rolled, tumbled, and twiddled his hats. Roey, Shai, Shaina, Kellin, and other jugglers presented a steal-the-club routine reminiscent of the steal-the-ball trick that Shai had initiated the first time the two troupes met five years earlier.

Hala and Einat pulled themselves up the silks to the top of

Circus Harmony's recessed ceiling, higher even than the hanging spotlights. The audience *oooooh*ed when Hala spun dramatically downward to just inches above the ring floor, caught at the last moment in the silk's cunning knots.

The performers rounded out their final finale with an eye-boggling, three-ring-in-one show ender.

"I'm very sorry to announce, for the last time," Jessica said, with a hitch in her voice, "the 2012 Galilee Arches."

Dive rolls. Handsprings. Back flips and back tucks. Two-Highs. He-Mans. Helicopters. Nothing But Nets. Death Drops.

On and on they went, the audience clapping and whooping in time to the music. The Galilee Circus and the Arches were so thoroughly integrated that, apart from their varied costumes and Hla's headscarf, it was hard to tell who was Arab or Jewish, Muslim or Christian, American or Israeli, foreign-born or local.

"The Galilee A-a-a-r-r-ches!" Jessica called as they scrambled into their final Pyramid. She announced the troupers' names as they flipped, skipped, and sprang out of the ring.

"Saying Goodbye"

Although Meghan had fun working with Hla, she had also found the two weeks with the Galilee Circus stressful. She had decided not to pursue circus as a career. "I'd rather continue my academic studies," Meghan said, "and see circus as something fun.... I don't think my body can handle the strenuous repercussions of that."

Rosa was disappointed; she had hoped Meghan would go to circus school. Instead, Meghan had applied to and been accepted by Lawrence University, her first choice, where she planned to study anthropology. "I want to learn everything about how people got to where they are and how they do things and why some people respond to situations one way and other people another way," she said.

Meghan would be leaving St. Louis in a month; she wanted to spend time with her school friends. As a result, she didn't join the Galilee Arches for all of their extra activities.

Max, Meghan, and Keaton perform in the Farewell Show

But one event was important for everyone to attend. The Farewell Show was an Arch tradition, presented every year for those who were graduating. The honorees perform tricks they've been working on, and their friends also perform, sometimes in ridiculous, clownish routines. Meghan and Keaton would both be honored.

Shaina did a solo ladder act. With the help of Alex Wallenda and Claire, Elliana spoofed Meghan and Keaton's Doughnut Drop trick. Then, Keaton and Kellin mocked each other, wearing footed jammies. With his fluffy hair clipped into a topknot, Kellin did a clown act with hula hoops. When the show was over, Meghan and Keaton carried out their final ritual—signing their names on the Arches' wall of graduates.

In the end, Meghan cried. "Saying goodbye to Rosa was the roughest part," she said.

You're Drafted!

Almost all Jewish citizens of Israel, male and female, are drafted into the IDF when they turn eighteen. Men serve for three years and women for almost two years. Officers and pilots serve longer terms.

Young people can be excused from military service if they are recognized as pacifists, if they are full-time religious students, or if they are "incompatible" with the military. Some choose to participate in a civilian service program.

The next morning, all of the troupers woke up extra early and went to Jessica's house to say goodbye to Keaton before he left for Montreal.

"It Was Going to Be My Last Tour"

After the Israelis returned to the Galilee, Shai would also be leaving the circus. Having graduated from high school, he was about to be inducted into the Israel Defense Forces. But because he was a pacifist, he was hoping to find a way to avoid serving.

"People don't think it's good not to join the army because then you're not contributing to the country," he said. "Personally, I don't care about the country. I don't see myself as Israeli or Jewish. Aside from that, I don't think violence can solve anything." Shai's plan was to misbehave and refuse to follow orders, so that the army would excuse him from service.

He had noticed Meghan's frustrations with spending so much time at circus rather than with her friends from school. He tried to make her feel better. "I think you're lucky," Shai told her, "because, for me, I have to join the army. A lot of my friends have battle jobs, which means you get a gun, and you go into battle when it's necessary. There's a chance I may never see them again.... You know that you'll be seeing [your friends] again. I don't."

Meghan understood Shai's point, but it didn't make her feel better. "It's a different situation," she said.

"I knew it was going to be my last tour," Shai said, "and it feels like a good conclusion for me.... Every trip, I would get emotional.... In 2012, I realized, I don't want to do it again. I don't want to get that emotional, in a negative way. And, I did it!"

"He has matured," Marc said. "This trip was much better than previous experiences with him.... He never really had a [strength]. In the past year or two, he's really gotten good at what he does.... The kid worked hard."

192

"You Know How to Hold Your Body"

Roey was pleased that he could take Keaton's place in Nothing But Net, diving through Meghan's leg during their few remaining shows. "In tumbling, after you practice a lot, you know how to feel your body, to know what its position is right now, and how to change it in the air," Roey said. "It gets really easy to do those kinds of tricks. If you do a dive roll through someone's leg, you don't want to relax; you'll go off and hit them.... After a few years, you know how to hold your body tight."

Roey also talked with Kellin about borrowing a few of his juggling stunts for shows back home. "You live in America," Roey told him. "We live in Israel. No one's going to notice if we take some of your tricks."

Roey and Yaron demonstrated the gags they did in Philadelphia. "Kellin said he was going to take them too," Roey said. "We're doing a switch." Jessica asked Roey if he'd like to return to St. Louis the following summer for a short circus internship.

Kellin also noticed how much the Galilee troupe had advanced. "It was easier to perform with them...," he said. "They didn't have to focus on what they were doing so they wouldn't mess up.

Jessica agreed. "They were really working like a troupe...a team," she said.

"You Have to Start Over"

The Arches were losing two key players—Meghan and Keaton. The year before, Iking, T-Roc, Elliana, and Claire had graduated.

Kellin was discouraged by the loss of these performers and worried about the future of the Arches. Jessica agreed—in part. "When you lose people, you have to start over," she acknowledged. "That's happening now with the Arches."

As usual, she had a plan. Shaina, Alex, and Max would be seniors in the fall. And, she added, "The seniors will bring up the freshmen."

And On They Go...

The English word "circus" derives from the ancient Greek word *kirkos*, meaning circle or ring. In Roman times, the word evolved into the Latin *circus*, which referred to a round or oval arena for performances and contests. Though often staged in rings, circuses don't merely go around in circles, repeating the same routines.

Like the word, circuses evolve. They change according to their performers' talents, interests, and skills. Circuses also adapt in response to the styles of other performers that they connect with around the world. This ability of circus to reinvent itself with each succeeding generation is a hallmark of this infinitely flexible and inclusive athletic and artistic enterprise.

The multiple ways it can be practiced and performed go on and on. The conversation within the worldwide circus family will go on and on too.

Turned on its edge, a circle becomes a wheel, rolling along. The Galilee Circus and the St. Louis Arches have shown that they can keep moving forward, continuing to attract young people who want to do extraordinary feats together regardless of religion, ethnicity, race, history, family income, or language. As they grow up, they will spin off into new worlds of their own creation, taking with them their confidence in themselves, their trust in and cooperation with each other, and their knowledge that they can fly together over previously unbridgeable divides.

Sababa!

When circus performers part, they typically say to one another, "See you down the road." They know that they'll see each other again, on some mud lot or in the next Circus Flora show or at an international workshop. The troupers of the Galilee Circus and the St. Louis Arches have traveled many roads since they separated in 2012. They still see each other, sometimes in person, more often on virtual highways.

Alexandra Gabliani

"Being with them [the Israelis] is the best feeling in the world, getting to know people who are so different and, somehow, still the same."

"There were times we couldn't communicate but it didn't really matter because there's a universal language between humans, and it's not necessarily through speech."

"You have to trust yourself. If you don't trust that you're going to catch someone, then you're not going to."

Alex left the Arches shortly after the Galilee Circus returned to Israel in August 2012. "I didn't leave because I didn't love the

The ring at Circus Harmony

people or because I didn't want to be a part," she said. She left because of what she felt was "pressure that was put on me to choose school or circus." Following high school graduation in 2013, Alex briefly attended the University of Kentucky. She returned to St. Louis, where she worked on hand balancing and trapeze with Rosa.

Hala Asadi

"We are like a big family that help each other and all the time together."

"I learned how to rely on myself and believe in me. I also learned to put my trust in other people to make the show work."

Hala is in the twelfth grade at Al-Bian Academy in Deir al-Asad. She continues to work on silks and intends to keep up with her Arab and Jewish friends from circus. After she completes university, Hala would like to help train younger circus troupers.

Hla Asadi

"We're with friends. She help me, I help her. Together. One hand."

"Arabs and Jewish people can be together. There's nothing impossible. You can do everything that you think is the right thing…."

Hla is in the eleventh grade at Al-Bian Academy in Deir al-Asad. She continues to develop her contortion skills and hopes to work as an English teacher and a contortion coach.

Kellin Quinn Hentoff-Killian

"I love juggling, and I would be happy to do that all the time.... There is an endless amount of possibilities you can do with every single prop and everyone has a potential to create something no one has ever seen before."

"Circus has changed me because I have something to do with my life.... I don't know where I want to go with circus but I know I want to do circus."

After he won the junior-level International Juggling Association Championship when he was sixteen years old, Kellin chose to compete at the senior level, against older and more experienced jugglers, including some of his idols. In the 2013 IJA competition, Kellin won both the Bronze Award and the People's Choice Award. Kellin graduated from high school in 2014 and joined his brother at *l'École nationale de cirque*. In addition, he formed a juggling troupe called Company McQuiggs.

Meghan Clark

"It's really cool when you begin to realize how body-oriented circus is, not language-oriented. To teach and work with people who do not understand us at all—that's a really cool thing to be exposed to."

"If I didn't go to circus.... I wouldn't have those friends that I have."

As a junior at Lawrence University, Meghan is majoring in anthropology. She has worked as a flexibility coach in a bilingual gymnastics program in Guatemala and served as an intern for the U.S. Department of State in Peru. Although Meghan still stretches, Rosa says that her back is not as strong as it was before she left for college.

Roey Shafran

"After I started playing in circus, I started playing in real life.... I have no boundaries."

"We worked together and taught the Arches to cooperate with people they don't know from around the world. That might have helped all the Arches who study in circus schools now."

"I don't think I would ever make Arab friends without the circus."

Roey continued both his physics and mathematics studies in high school and his juggling work with the Galilee Circus. He also interned with the Arches for three weeks in 2013. During his senior year of high school, he and a team of fellow students won Israel's Intel International Science and Engineering Fair with a mechanical system that automatically responds to oil spills, which they presented in Los Angeles, California. Following graduation in 2014, he was inducted into the Israel Defense Forces.

Shai Ben Yosef

"Circus is not about competition. It's about art and getting better. The objective is not to beat the other people at what you do."

"What I notice when I'm teaching is the kids now don't care about the Jewish-Arab thing. They're kids. They don't know it's a really powerful thing."

Following his induction into the Israel Defense Forces, Shai refused to participate in training. He was examined by military personnel and doctors and threatened with imprisonment. After five months, he was released from duty and received permission to do alternative service by working at the circus. He now attends the *FLIC Scuola di Circo*, a circus preparatory school in Turin, Italy.

Shaina Hughes

"[Working with the Galilee Circus] has taught the Arches not to be prejudiced against other races because you don't know what they're going through."

"Circus gave me a confidence boost. I can do things that other people can't do, and circus makes me feel happy whenever I come here."

During her senior year of high school, Shaina auditioned for both *l'École de cirque de Québec* and *l'École nationale de cirque* but was not accepted by either. After graduation in 2013, she left the Arches, hoping to attend community college. She has been unable to complete her degree, however, and worked in Circus Harmony's snack bar. Shaina would still like to perform for UniverSOUL Circus but does not currently have an act to present. Her son was born in July 2014.

Sidney Akeem ("Iking") Bateman

"I see the whole big old world, not just the small place I live in."

"Circus will push you to be the best you can be at anything."

"They taught me circus skills but they were teaching me other things too. About life."

"Without boxes, borders or boundaries, I built dreams."

In July 2013, Iking set a Guinness World Record by flipping forty-two consecutive back handsprings. After majoring in Chinese hoops and diabolo, Iking graduated from *l'École nationale de cirque* in 2014. He is traveling the world with a new theatrical creation of the famed Canadian circus company, *Les 7 Doigts de la Main* (The 7 Fingers of the Hand).

Jessica Hentoff and Circus Harmony

"Teaching children from different cultures to stand on each other's shoulders may seem like a strange way to promote cooperation and communication, but it's the technique we use."

"The Arches have given the Galilee Circus a growth hormone."

"I am an artist for social justice."

Jessica opened the Circus Harmony Flying Trapeze Center in St. Louis's former Union Station train depot in 2014. That summer, after scrambling yet again for funds, the Arches returned to Israel—this time with the next generation of troupers. During their visit, a ground war broke out in Gaza between Israel and Hamas, a militant anti-Israeli Palestinian group. The Federal Aviation Administration halted flights between the United States and Israel, stranding the flying kids. They spent an additional week with their partners in the Galilee.

A week after their return, a white policeman shot and killed an unarmed black teenager in Ferguson, a largely black municipality on the north side of St. Louis, near Jessica's home. Protests by infuriated citizens continued for nearly two weeks, drawing tear gas from police, curfews, the National Guard, civil rights leaders, and federal officials.

Jessica's daughter, Elliana, joined Ringling as its youngest human cannonball, then returned to St. Louis, where she teaches and performs at the Circus Harmony Flying Trapeze Center.

Marc Rosenstein and the Galilee Circus

"There are no losers here."

"Circus will not bring peace to the Middle East.... It can demonstrate, to a wide audience, that what appears to be impossible is indeed possible."

"The circus is a drop in the bucket. But we hope the drops will accumulate."

In addition to maintaining its partnership with the St. Louis Arches, the Galilee Circus has also developed relationships with youth circuses in Holland and Germany.

Troupers and their families continue to hold their annual joint picnic—a rare and, at the same time, unremarkable event. Marc hopes the Galilee Circus can establish a permanent, dedicated home as well as satellite social circuses in other towns in Israel.

Marc retired as the executive director of the Galilee Foundation for Value Education in September 2013. More than 700 Arabs and Jews jointly honored him at a special circus performance. The mixture of performers and audience is "not an everyday occurrence around here," he said. "In fact, I haven't yet met anyone who has ever experienced it."

Author's Note

Why I Wrote This Book

The first time I visited Israel, in 1969, I was struck by its rich diversity. Most obvious was the diversity of the people—their clothes, languages, skin tones, foods. The diversity of the terrain was also remarkable. This tiny country seemed to hold a miniature sample of almost every land form in the United States—deserts, tropical lushness, canyons, mountains, flatlands, ocean, lakes.

As an American, I take pride in our country's ability to accommodate our varied populations and appreciate our landscapes. And I despair when we segregate or assault people who look different from us and when we damage our natural resources. Yet, that visit made me realize that America seems almost homogeneous compared to a country with the wide variety of cultures and landforms that rub against each other in such close proximity in Israel.

In June 2010, during one of my many return visits to Israel, I was casting about for a book topic. Thanks to my niece, Sarai Brachman Shoup, and a colleague of hers, Batya Kallus, I learned about the Galilee Circus. *A kids' circus*, I thought, *how fun!* Batya drove me from Jerusalem to a gym near Shorashim where we spent part of a day talking with Rabbi Marc Rosenstein and watching kids teeter on stilts and attempt backward rolls.

Fun, yes, but, at the time, I had no idea what I was getting into. (Authors often say this. Why don't we learn?!) Until I met Marc, I'd never heard of youth circus, let alone social circus. Through him, I got to know Jessica Hentoff and the St. Louis Arches, who showed me the meaning of social circus in America.

To decide whether or not to write a book about youth circus, I first had to figure out whether circus is materially different from other kids' activities. Fine books for young readers have been written about soccer, for instance, and drama. Did circus warrant treatment as well?

To find out, I traveled to Saratoga Springs, New York; Sarasota, Florida; Williamstown, Massachusetts; Chicago, Illinois; Boston, Massachusetts; and St. Louis, Missouri, to observe nearly a dozen youth circuses in action. As I hope you've seen in the stories about the Galilee Circus and Circus Harmony, I concluded that this activity is very different, indeed, from typical sports and arts programs for children. And when I tried to juggle, walk a tightwire, balance on a globe, roll down silks, and leap off a mini-tramp, I was completely convinced! *Circus is hard.*

The incident, though, that persuaded me to write this book was a conversation I had with Hla Asadi in July 2012, over two years after I had started the research. The Galilee Circus was visiting Circus Harmony in St. Louis. Because City Museum is packed to its boisterous ten-story brim with equipment and miscellany for kids to play on, the only place we could find to sit and talk was on the floor, beneath the clothing racks of a secondhand store tucked into a corner on the fourth story of the building.

Although I had traveled many times to Israel (and even lived there for a semester) and had visited Egypt and Jordan, I was still struggling to understand why activities that involve both Arabs and Jews, especially young ones, are so rare. I asked Hla, "Are people upset that you're involved in an Arab-Jewish program?"

Her response stunned me. With exasperation and defiance, she replied, "*Nobody* could understand. Even you. Could *you* understand that Arab and Jewish people could be together?"

From Hla's perspective, no one anywhere could possibly conceive that Arabs and Jews could work and play together. At that moment, I knew I needed to help make the notion understandable and acceptable that not only Jews and Arabs but also blacks, whites, Muslims, Christians—all kids—can get along. And that circus is an especially enchanting means in which to do so.

My editor, the indefatigable and deeply insightful Kathy Landwehr, had joined me on that trip to St. Louis. When she offered to publish a book about these two circuses, I enthusiastically accepted—still having little idea of what I was getting into. Two months later, I made my way to Karmiel and Deir al-Asad where Roey's, Hala's, and Hla's families generously hosted me while I peppered them with personal questions. After over two years of initial research, my journeys into the worlds of circus were just beginning.

How I Wrote This Book

Almost all of the research I conducted for *Watch Out for Flying Kids* came from primary sources. The preponderance of the information, especially about the nine featured troupers, the two circus directors, and the coaches, came from personal interviews— more than 120 hours' worth—which I transcribed and sorted into a database. Following our initial in-person conversations, we used whichever technology they preferred—telephone (Shaina, Meghan, and Jessica), e-mail (Iking, Kellin, Dagan, Marc, Sariya, Veronika, and Warren), Facebook video (Shai), Facebook messaging (Alex and Roey), and Skype (Hla and Hala, when they, a functioning computer, a reliable internet connection, and a translator were all available simultaneously).

In addition, I admit that I trawled their Facebook pages and YouTube channels; groveled for photographs and videos; and unearthed e-mails, newsletters, publicity materials, television newscasts, brochures, and blogs, in a variety of languages. Photographs of the Galilee Circus were particularly challenging to obtain. As an after-school program, the group was not so thoroughly documented as were the high-flying Arches. Nevertheless, I especially enjoyed observing and filming countless enthralling hours of circus practices and performances by both circuses and others I observed.

Although the troupers were busy teenagers with far more pressing demands than answering the impertinent questions of a children's author, everyone generously shared their stories, even if they sometimes did so on a timeline that differed from the one I had anticipated.

To obtain background information, I also read books, magazines, and articles written for adults on Judaism, Islam, the history and politics of Israel, the history and politics of St. Louis, and, of course, the history and practice of circus arts.

Despite this extensive research, I fret that there may be holes in the stories I tell of the troupers and their circuses. I also fear that, as an American Jew, I might have missed or misunderstood perspectives that Hala and Hla, in particular, tried to convey. For these gaps, I extend my apologies and thank each one for allowing me to enter and share their lives.

For young readers who would like to learn more about youth circus, I suggest the following accessible resources:

Circus Harmony and the St. Louis Arches
www.circusharmony.org

Galilee Circus
www.eng.makom-bagalil.org.il/galileecircus

"Circus Kids," a documentary film about the Arches' trip to Israel in 2007, by Alexandra Lipsitz, available through Circus Harmony

American Youth Circus Organization (AYCO)
www.americanyouthcircus.org

Circus Fans of America
www.circus4youth.org

Watch Out for Flying Kids!
www.watchoutforflyingkids.com

Acknowledgments

In addition to the extraordinary young performers and circus directors to whom *Watch Out for Flying Kids* is dedicated, I bombarded many other people with my persistent and often personal questions. Not being conversant in Arabic, Hebrew, or Circus, I am immeasurably indebted to the following people for serving as my generous and candid guides into their worlds.

For background into circus: Warren Adams Bacon, Amy Cohen, Jacqueline Davis, Janet Davis, Maribeth Joy, Chauncey Kroner, Cecil MacKinnon, Rob Mermin, Marc Miller, Laura Ricci, Alex Wallenda, and Troy and Sara Wunderle.

For translations from Arabic and insights into Israeli Arab perspectives: Salam Abu Zeid, Hasan Asadi, and Iman Kadach.

For their experiences with the Galilee Circus, insights into Israeli Arab perspectives, and life in Deir al-Asad: Manal Akawi, Gada and Yousef Asadi, Sameha and Aziz Asadi, Mahmoun Assadi, Saeed Assaf, Sawsan Bakri, Ali Hasarme, Manar Khalil, Mahmoud Omar, Ahmad Sanallah, and Samer Sanallah.

For their experiences with the Galilee Circus, insights into Israeli Jewish perspectives, and life in Atzmon and Karmiel: Hana and Tom Ben Yosef, Yaron and Alex Davidovich, Chassia Homsky, Shirel Mondrik, Einat Opalin, Orly and Hanoch Shafran, and Nir Topper.

For their experiences with Circus Harmony and insights into its members: Linda Bateman, Richard Bonomo, Angie Elkins (now deceased), Jacqueline Gabliani, Elena Greene, Keaton Hentoff-Killian, "Big" Donald Hughes, "Lil" Donald Hughes, Tanner Latham, Alexandra Lipsitz, Reginald P. Moore (in sad memoriam), Max and Susan Pepose, Diane Rankin, Mei Ling Robin, Terrance ("T-Roc") Robinson, Karen Schellin, and Renaldo ("Junior") Williams.

For coaching advice: Dagan Dishbak, Gilad Finkel, Elliana Hentoff-Killian, Sarah Herr, Richard Kennison, John Krueger,

206

Veronika Reichard, Debbie Rosenberg, Sariya Saabye, and Rosa Yagaantsetseg.

For insights into Arab-Jewish relations and programs in Israel: Batya Kallus, Pnina Lahav, Ofer Lior, Hedva Livnat, Moriel Rothman, Enid Schatz, Sarai Brachman Shoup, Tsafy Simons, and Sigalit Ur.

For transliteration from Hebrew and Arabic to English: Yuval Edrey and Waseem Hajo.

As always, I am also deeply indebted to the following people whom I am proud and honored to consider my partners in writing and in life.

For (deservedly) shredding and helping me reassemble this project: Victoria Coe, Hillary deBaun, Joe Lawlor, Patrice Sherman, Donna Janell Bowman, Carole Buckman, Mary Reilly, and Polly Robertus.

For mentoring my writing: the many stellar writers of nonfiction for young people, particularly Peggy Thomas, who critiqued an early version.

For believing that this little engine could: Kathy Landwehr, Margaret Quinlin, and Erin Murphy. For designing an exuberant book: Nicki Carmack.

And, for everything of value in my life: My thoroughly splendid family—Sandy, Meira, Marc, Rebecca, Ella, Rachel, Ariel, Sarah, and Eli.

Photo Credits

Aya Aa'amar
196 (Hla Asadi)

Hala Asadi
196 (Hala Asadi)

Hana Ben Yosef
30

Richard Bonomo
66, 74, 75, 76

Brenda Clark
11

Dagan Dishbak
84, 111, 112, 117, 143, 145, 147, 167, 168, 170, 173, back cover (Hla Asadi)

Alex Gabliani
195

Jessica Hentoff
8, 13, 14, 18, 20, 25, 44, 49, 53, 55, 57, 61, 64, 68, 69, 73, 78, 79, 86, 90, 91, 92, 98, 99, 100, 101, 102, 103, 104, 105, 121, 122, 125, 128, 129, 133, 134, 149, 152, 155, 157, 160, 161, 175, 182, 187, 189, 191, 195 (Kellin Quinn Hentoff-Killian), front cover (Pyramid), back cover (Iking Bateman)

Joyce Howard
48

Shaina Hughes
127, 199

Tanner Latham
29, 35, 135, 137, 139, 198 (Roey Shafran), front cover (Hla Asadi and Hala Asadi, Roey Shafran), back cover (hands)

Cynthia Levinson
2, 23, 27, 38, 41, 52, 59, 81, 96, 109, 110, 119, 124, 142, 148, 165, 171, 177, 179, 180, 184, 198 (Shai Ben Yosef), 199 (Iking Bateman), front cover (Iking Bateman)

David Mitchell
47, 150, 200

Dorota Odzierejko
197

Diane Rankin
9

Tami Rosenstein
201

Matthew Saabye
106

Serrick Photo
4

Al Vitale
131

Jeanne Vogel
6

The artwork on page 53 was created by Mary Englebreit.

208

Index

210